Paddling Back to Us

A Journey into Wildness on Connected Waterways

By **Kay Deborah Linley**

This book is dedicated to the adventurous nature that resides within each and every one of us.

May these words and images nurture your strength, bravery, and willingness to explore your inner and outer worlds on this solo journey collective.

Copyright © 2022 by Kay Linley

All rights reserved. No part of this book may be reproduced or transmitted in any form or by any means, electronic or mechanical, including photocopying, recording, or by any information storage and retrieval system, without permission in writing from the author.

ISBN 978-1-7781898-0-7

First Nation Acknowledgment

I recognize and give thanks to all of the First Nations whose traditional lands and waters I travelled during my kayaking pilgrimage. It is your ongoing stewardship of the land and water that provides all of us with the opportunity to experience these profound natural places today and into the future.

Through the wind, she beckoned me,

clattering amidst the poplar leaves and dancing with the wild arnica.

I followed her voice down a narrow path

shrouded by balsam fir, with trunks wrapped in pockets of healing oils.

Then she dispersed, stretching out along the wide arms of the beach.

I sat down and melted into her warmth

and remained so still that I began moving again.

With the ebb and flow of the waves,

I breathed into a world of belonging.

Magnetic North

"I don't have space for you anymore." The mist of my breath danced along the column of light from my headlamp and into Jeremy's face before being consumed by the thick ice fog. It was -40 degrees Celsius and pitch-black outside, but I could still see the space behind Jeremy's eyes deepen from the impact of my words. Jeremy went quiet and stood absolutely still, as though he was reserving his energy for the inevitable, tough conversations ahead. Then, he turned away and shone his headlamp down the dark, narrow trail—its light unveiling only a small portion of the path ahead of us, before being swallowed by the abyss of the sub-arctic winter.

I was on a rampage, slashing and burning the parts of my life that meant the most to me. I bowed out of social events and stopped spending time with friends, then I started to abandon my passion projects and hobbies, like painting and writing. This time, it was my relationship that made the chopping block. The overwhelming stress from my work and living situation was taking me into a dark mental state. If I did not make some serious changes, I would lose the remaining things I loved. I felt a bit young to be going through a burn-out, only thirty-four, but it was clear I could no longer continue living the life I had created. My body and psyche were screaming for a different way of being.

Seven years prior, in 2011, I moved north to Dawson City, Yukon, over 2,400 kilometres away from my immediate family. Unlike my sisters, who returned to our hometown of Nelson, British Columbia after their adventures, I left to create a life for myself in the north. Similar to Dawson City, The City of Nelson was established in the late 1800s by explorers searching for gold deposits. Though they didn't strike it lucky for gold, they did find a copper-silver deposit, which began a rush in the region and led to the establishment of the town. Even the geography of Nelson and Dawson City was similar, they were both small towns sandwiched against waterfront and surrounded by densely forested, rolling mountains. So, even though I ventured far from my hometown, a similarity travelled with me.

People asked me why I moved so far away. It felt like I was being drawn northward by a massive magnet. I couldn't stop talking about it until one day my oldest sister Ruth joked, "Well, maybe you should move up there so you stop talking about it so much."

Leaving my hometown felt a bit like running, but I couldn't seem to overcome the discomfort of living there after a difficult childhood. There were too many memories surrounding the disintegration and instability of my upbringing. While my sisters found a way to live in the midst of where those were borne, something in me needed the unknown to recreate my life. And so, taking my sister's prompting, move north I did.

In 2016, I purchased an off-grid cabin on a small chunk of land across from Dawson City on the other side of the Yukon River. True to my character, I chose a home that confronted me with extreme challenges. The cabin was only accessible at certain times of the year because of the Yukon River. In the summer months, when the ferry was operating, I could get home from work relatively easily. But every spring and fall, there was neither a ferry nor a stable ice bridge for crossing. I would have to scrounge and find temporary lodging on town-side so that I could continue to go to work.

Once winter hit, I could move back home after a reliable ice bridge had formed. But unfortunately, as soon as I had bought my property, the ice stopped "jamming" in front of town, rendering the location of the ice bridge inconsistent. Sometimes the ice would jam downriver from town, so my hike home was extremely long compared to a direct shot from one ferry landing to the other. After a long day's work as Land and Resources Manager for the Tr'ondëk Hwëch'in First Nation, it could take me and my dog Mya, while she was still alive, up to an hour and a half to hike home in the dark.

There were only a few hours of daylight in the depths of winter and I didn't have electricity at home, so for many months my world felt limited to the light cast from my headlamp and kerosene lanterns. In addition to the dark, my home lacked insulation and the woodstove was too small for the space, especially when it was not being tended during the longer days I was working. The temperature in Dawson could dip to -50 degrees Celsius, so it didn't take long for my house to freeze. When I got home, my first order of business was to light the fire in the woodstove and melt some snow for hot water bottles to put in my bed. I kept my one-piece snowsuit on most evenings and even slept with it on during the coldest nights. Every night around 2am, I would wake to a dying fire and dash downstairs from the loft to quickly stoke and load the woodstove to last another few hours.

I knew I wasn't a complete victim of my circumstance as my personality played a key role in the developments of my life. Choosing to move to Dawson, and choosing to buy the cabin on the property I did, meant I needed to navigate a particular and unique set of hardships that many folks do not. I had always made choices that led me down the harder, less-travelled road, though I couldn't place where this character trait came from or when it started. That said, early memories from my childhood reveal how I grappled with this seemingly odd behaviour even back then.

I can still recall, for example, how at six years old, I decided to ride my small, red bicycle down one of my hometown's steepest back alleys. It was a decent bike, but the brakes were a bit old and needed some work. As the gravel popped and snapped under my whizzing tires, I realized that at the bottom of the hill, there was a sharp turn. My six-year-old self also realized that, to make this turn, I would have to use my touchy breaks, and this would certainly mean wiping-out. The alternative was to continue cycling straight at the bottom of the hill and launch over the grassy bank into the unknown. In that split second, I chose the potential of the unknown rather than the pain I could imagine. My bike wheels burned through the thick grass, then spun futilely in mid-air as I experienced weightlessness. Then the bike fell away from my limbs as we both came hurtling down the fifteen-foot drop, crashing as two mangled heaps onto the gravel road below. Shards of small angular pebbles penetrated my left kneecap ripping a deep sore over the entire joint, and the once soft part of my left thumb welled with blood, like a hollowed-out puddle. In hindsight, perhaps a graze from using my not so good breaks to make the sharp turn would have been the wiser option.

While it's easy to speculate about and even make judgements on my childhood choices, the wisdom of my decision to live as I did in the north as an adult was still being revealed. In addition to the challenging living arrangements I had chosen for myself, the job I had applied for was no walk in the park either. The local First Nation, the Tr'ondëk Hwëch'in, hired me on as their Land and Resources Manager. My job was to help them steward their Traditional Territory, an area of about 50,000 square kilometres. I was honoured to have been awarded the important position, but the workload was immense. Given the territory's suspected and known wealth of gold deposits, it was all I could do to keep up with the constant barrage of individual and corporate interests in prospecting and establishing mines in the region. It was as if the Gold Rush of the late 1800's had never ended.

With what remained of my energy, I would try and find a spare moment to spend with my new boyfriend Jeremy. Our relationship was less than a year old so we didn't live together yet, but we would have visits where I would spend the night at his place. While my long days were spent responding to the continued, burgeoning pressures at work, at night, I would lay wide awake next to him. While he slept peacefully, my mind raced frantically in a feeble attempt to ward off the imminent threat of the all-consuming Empire. Would I be able to keep track of the constant barrage of mining applications? Would I be able to catch the ones most critical to the First Nation's interests and well-being? The applications and licenses I was responsible for overseeing felt like grains of sand slipping through my fingers and accumulating across the territory. How could I choose which ones to triage for in-depth review and comment when the land as a functioning whole was the critical value? Each development added up and together across the landscape they could have lasting impact on the animals, plants and the water that the First Nation relied upon to practice their rights now and into the future. There was also an underlying impact to the First Nation's beliefs and way of life from the largely unfettered development throughout their Traditional Territory.

I felt a weight bearing down on my chest from a sense of responsibility far beyond my job description. The goals of my position felt untenable given the antiquated legal structure we worked within and I could sense a much larger driving force behind the mining industry from our societal addiction to consume. In addition, the very task of caring for the environment struck close to home as I had developed a close relationship with the natural world in my childhood. Nature was a place I would retreat to for its unconditional love, so I felt indebted to the environment for all its years of service during my childhood challenges. I also felt a deep responsibility to the First Nation, as a newcomer from colonial origins. Meanwhile, I missed my best friend, Mya, the Siberian husky who had entered my life six years earlier, and whose sudden departure the previous summer still left me with waves of grief that would catch me unaware in the midst of all else going on in my life.

As my psyche was consumed with these worries and fears and with the lingering ache from losing my trusted companion, Mya, my body also started to display curious symptoms. In addition to heart palpitations and Raynaud's-like symptoms in my hands, a mysterious rash appeared on my left cheek, in a perfect circle. I chalked it up to ring worm and picked up some cream from the doctor, hoping for a quick fix. It seemed like the remedy worked, and the red mark went away, at least for a while.

Under the strain of my degrading mind and my unsettled body, I began lashing out at the person closest to me, Jeremy. In a desperate call for help, I threw my anguish at him, so that he might understand how much I was hurting. I was short and impatient with him and overly critical in our exchanges. Sometimes I would interrogate him, trying to pin fault as though he were responsible for the state of our society. When I projected my pain and anger onto him, he would shut down, both emotionally and physically, into an almost paralyzed state. He couldn't respond to me and embodied such a quietness that I could hear him swallow uncomfortably. He seemed genuinely afraid of me, like I was some kind of monster. This left me feeling disgusted with myself and wanting to escape my own skin.

After many weeks of this distressing dynamic, one evening when I was in a calmer state, Jeremy must have felt like he had nothing to lose for him to stick his neck out with a bold proposal. He looked over at me with deep concern across the dining room table. "Babe, how about a break from Dawson?"

I looked up at him after downing a mouthful of mashed potatoes, shifting in my seat as if I were on trial. I felt beat-up and defeated and wanted an ounce of relief just as much as Jeremy did. *At this point, I'm willing to try anything,* I thought. "Okay, but where would we go?"

He finished chewing his own mouthful of food and then swallowed deeply. For someone who had a relaxed temperament and let things slide off his back most of the time, he seemed to be bearing a weight of his own. "We could go to my farm in Atlin? Spend the summer growing veggies?"

"Oh?" I had been to the land with him once before over a long weekend, and remembered feeling calmer there. "I do love those big trees down there by the cabin. A beautiful spot."

"Yeah, a bit of heaven on earth. It could be just what you need," Jeremy added, with just enough conviction that the words made it past my ears and into the part of me that could hear him. "The work would be the opposite of what you're doing now."

"It sure would be." I let myself imagine us growing vegetables together, surrounded by nature. It seemed romantic.

"Maybe a little time with your hands in the dirt would help?" Jeremy reached over and rested his hand over mine before squeezing it gently.

"Maybe." I lifted my eyebrows to expand my weary eyes and tensed my cheeks forcing my thin lips into a smile. I could feel Jeremy's desperation in trying to improve the situation we currently found ourselves in and felt guilty about being such a stress case.

At this point, my anxiety was unrelenting and it felt like there was no escaping. I couldn't sleep by night and was hypervigilant by day. My chest felt so constricted I had forgotten what it felt like to inhale deeply. In fact, part of me was so used to being constantly on edge, that it felt like a new normal; or maybe it was just an amplified state of what for me was an "old normal." Perhaps starting as a child, who quickly learned to guard herself in a conflict and trauma-filled family setting, I had become used to this way of relating with the world. Not only was my anxiety a result from my childhood protections, it was also a normalized state I had accepted from the reoccurring exposure. Part of me was unsure whether I could unlearn it, or in the least try something different.

I looked into Jeremy's begging eyes and could see I wasn't the only one I needed to be brave for.

The Heart Decides

That spring, after eight hours of driving, we pulled up to the T-intersection at the entrance to Atlin; I had decided to take a leave of absence from my job with the First Nation and agreed with Jeremy's proposition to try my hand at gardening. The small town, located in the northwestern corner of BC, was nestled alongside a large lake lined with impressive mountains. There were two small grocery stores, a post office, and a hotel that looked closed. With a population of maybe 400 people at the busiest time of year, the town felt depressed and wanting of its earlier Gold Rush heyday. That said, some of the historic buildings were still standing and well-looked-after. It reminded me a little of Dawson.

Instead of turning in, we turned left away from the town's centre and headed into the bush. *We sure share a love for remote wilderness,* I thought, as we continued down a long, winding and bumpy road for another forty minutes, far beyond the last house and electricity pole. We had to drive slowly with my small travel trailer in tow. This trailer would be our accommodation for the summer because the cabin on the property was too small for the two of us and our three dogs. When we finally got to Jeremy's stretch of land, I could barely move from exhaustion. I exited the dust-covered truck, let the excited dogs out of the cab, and then hobbled into a large clearing overlooking a small river. The surroundings appeared even wilder than the area around my off-grid cabin in Dawson. Directly across the river, vast tracts of untouched wilderness spread out beyond the visible horizon. I revelled in a moment of appreciation for this intact land, without a trace of human meddling.

A pain sank from my throat into my heart, as I was reminded of the important work and people I had left behind. *Oh God, please let this be a place of healing, not a place for me to remember the loss.* A feeling of weighty guilt plummeted onto my shoulders as I judged myself for having chosen my well-being over the integrity of the land and the protection of the First Nation's rights and interests. I had become very attached to the people and empathized deeply with their efforts to look after the land, water and animals. I rubbed my eyes and re-focused my gaze on the overgrown garden at the bottom of the slope. *Hopefully the dirt will save me.*

But instead of embracing the relaxed lifestyle of hobby gardening and living on the land, I purchased some whiteboards and calendars and made lists upon lists of all the tasks that needed to be done. I recorded when and where everything was planted, how it was planted, and from what seed stock each new sprout sprang. Planning the garden down to the smallest detail and keeping busy with charting and recording the minutia day-to-day was my way of maintaining control, which I clung to for fear of losing myself to the abyss of endless sky, green brush, and trees along with the deep quiet around us. It especially helped me to distract myself from the waves of regret I experienced in having made the decision to step away from my position with the First Nation; though I'd come to that decision only after reaching my own outer limits, I felt like I was letting my employers down along with the land I helped them manage.

"You can relax a little you know," Jeremy looked over at me as I uncapped the dry erase marker and drew another column on the whiteboard for "Things Not to Forget."

I turned, held up the marker in front of me like a wand, and scowled back at him. "What do you mean? I thought you wanted a functional garden. It has to be planned you know. We need to keep track of what worked and what didn't so we can learn for next year. These things don't just happen on their own you know." I immediately went back to my calendar and jotted down, "Till earth and plant red onions."

Like a drug addict trying to manage withdrawal symptoms, I so desperately worked to get a fix of familiar adrenaline by re-immersing myself in another kind of busy. I was terrified of what might surface emotionally, now that I had slowed down and had time to catch up with myself. *Can I withstand the embarrassment of not being able to handle the stress of the job? Or the doubt about whether I've made the right decision? Seems I've simply traded my work stress for the stress of uncertainty.*

Over the course of our first month at the farm, I slowly released my grip and heeded Jeremy's advice. I began to feel a little safer and supported by the nature all around us. As the wild animals, birds, insects and plants consistently went about their business without judging my life drama, it felt a little easier to let go. Even the seeds I planted didn't seem to mind that their gardener was at a loss with her life, and most started growing regardless. Our three dogs shared their love of the wilderness with me while we walked together in the diverse, mature forest. As I eased into our peaceful surroundings, I noticed how my connection with our dogs deepened and it was easier for me to communicate with them and understand their needs. It reminded me a little of the profound connection I had had with Mya, my Siberian husky who had passed away the year before. Jeremy's calm presence and demonstration of a relaxed lifestyle, also helped me unravel just a little bit more. He genuinely listened to me as I offloaded my mixed feelings of having left my work with the First Nation. Though it was difficult for him as an outsider to fully understand how complicated the work had been, he consoled my sense of loss and tried to put my uncertainty to rest by reminding me that I was simply on a break and could always return to the work, or decide to do different work once the summer and our gardening season was over. I began replacing the list writing of every last detail for "Project Hobby Farm," with mountain gazing, dog walking and weeding the garden.

Because I was no longer producing large outputs of work, the external recognition of my usefulness was not there anymore to fill in the growing void where my self-worth used to be. Bit by bit, I came to realize how much I had tied my self-worth to outside qualifications, rather than an inner knowing and feeling of peace. Even with this unfolding understanding, I still grappled with the ego-hit now I was essentially a nobody in essentially the middle of nowhere.

The dramatic transition from being on edge, to being nowhere really at all, left me feeling disoriented. My mind felt foggy and my once sharp thoughts became dull and formless. Without the incessant external pressure I was used to, my brain couldn't operate the same.

Great, and now I'm useless, I admonished myself.

I knew deep down the whole reason I came to the farm was to unwind, heal, and find my way back to me, but I hadn't foreseen how uncomfortable the process would be, not only for my hardwired brain, but also for my habituated body. Given the opportunity to relax, my body first needed to express its anger from the years of pushing myself to the brink of collapse with unsustainable work habits. The skin sores that had visited me in Dawson came screaming back, erupting in the most sensitive areas, rendering me disgusted as I cringed in horrifying judgment of my impurity. My hands broke out in unsightly, itchy, painful sores that extended up along the topsides of my fingers. The breakouts would start in small, red bumps on my fingers and crescendo into flushed, fluid-filled welts across the entire backs of my hands. My hands themselves were icy-cold all the time and their colouring would vary dramatically from white to red. Small red dots appeared across my belly and rough, cracked eczema pocks developed along my forearms. As if this wasn't enough, a prickly patch of shingles also flared up on the tender skin just below my left armpit. I knew it was shingles, because I had had an anomalous experience with the virus and rash when I was a child. To top it off, the curious skin rash on my left cheek returned, this time in the shape of a butterfly wing. The irony of this did not slip past me as I sank further into a state of heavy, irritated stillness on the small patch of earth Jeremy and I inhabited.

This wasn't the first time my body had cried wolf. I remembered when I was twenty-eight during my oil patch days, when I held a position as seismic surveyor in northern Alberta; after a few months surveying exploration grid lines in the dead of winter, hundreds of itinerant hives had appeared all over my body, and my nose wouldn't stop bleeding. I recalled while visiting my sister in southern BC over Christmas, going to the hospital to get checked out to make sure I wasn't having a serious allergic reaction to something. The nurse who attended to me confirmed it was an allergy, but not from a substance.

"Oh, Honey," she said, "you've been working yourself too hard!"

True to form, I was not prepared to address my addiction at that time. Instead, again and again, I shut my body down by choosing extreme busyness at all costs. Mentally, I had disguised this lifestyle choice as a kind of "getting ahead;" besides, this was what society prescribed for personal success. In school, they taught us the best way to realize a fulfilled life was to go back to school and become somebody, like one of those highly admired doctors, lawyers, politicians or cut-throat business people on TV. I mean, it was the only way to afford the very many things the media taught us we needed for social acceptance and love, or at least romantic love. We must work hard, but that's still not enough. We need to work harder to be the brightest, the best, and the most successful. The other driving force for my work addiction was my memories of growing up on welfare. I was determined to claw my way up and out of first-world poverty into middle-class, and in my mind, this required an incessant striving for success. But the reality and result of ignoring my body's insistent messages, and pushing myself to extremes, was anything but success; rather these behaviours spun a thick paste that functioned to seal my deeply imbedded traumas within me so they would not re-surface, well, at least not for a while. The full-body eruption that arose now, once I was in the deep quiet of tending the earth with my partner far from the pressures of work and civilization, marked the beginning of a transformative shift I was about to undergo.

With my winged cheek, welted fingers and icy-cold hands, I made the drive into Atlin, where I paid a visit to the small community's medical clinic. The doctor looked at me curiously, shook his head gently, and asked, "Why so stressed?"

It was hard for me to answer him. Remote farm life with Jeremy should have been offering me the reprieve I needed. I wondered, was it the transition from high-pressure mental-managerial work to working the land that my body was reacting to? Or was I experiencing a delayed reaction to the stress I had previously been under while slowly toppling under the unceasing barrage of outsiders' interests in the First Nation Traditional Territory. Or was I crumbling under the weight of my own internal conflict about how the land was being handled? Did my body feel somehow unsafe now that I had removed myself from that acute pressure? Had the pressure I'd been under kept me "safe"? And, if so, from what? These thoughts and questions flooded my mind as I paused before finally attempting to answer the physician's query.

"Uh, well, I recently left a stressful job. Maybe I'm reacting to that?"

The doctor didn't seem surprised that the stress from the work I had been doing could have caused the outbreaks. Possible cause aside, he looked at the backsides of my fingers and hands and then fixated on my cheek decoration. He squinted as he moved my chin back and forth under the fluorescent light to get a better look.

"That rash looks suspect . . . possibly lupus." He wrote up some blood work orders to test for autoimmune diseases, and told me to make an appointment with the hospital in Whitehorse.

Concerned by the potential that I had a serious illness, I left the clinic reeling. *What is going on? Is my body trying to destroy itself?* With no definite answers, I returned to the farm and to planting potatoes. Although I tried to focus on the day-to-day chores to stay grounded, my nagging feelings of being lost and losing even more control took precedence, tearing away that very ground from underneath me. Then frustration set in. Was I not trying to help my body and mind by making the decision to take this leave and try peace and quiet for a change? Then anger at my seemingly ungrateful body. Then a flattening fear. *What if I have lupus? Or worse? I might become debilitated, incapacitated, and impure with disease.* I had always prided myself with good health up until the symptoms started. *Who will I become if I am diagnosed? How will this affect my lifestyle? And my relationship with Jeremy?*

By bringing me to Atlin, Jeremy had hoped my stresses would dwindle, not manifest into health problems. During his childhood, Jeremy spent far too much time in hospitals enduring treatments and surgeries for severe Crohn's Disease. He told me he got frustrated with adults who had health issues for the first time, because he felt they over-dramatized them. With his experience of serious disease at a young age, minor health concerns like the ones I was experiencing seemed just that, minor. He figured if it wasn't a completely debilitating issue, then it wasn't that bad. Because of his somewhat dismissive reaction, and because my symptoms were so nebulous and nondescript, I wondered if Jeremy thought it was all in my head. He seemed troubled about how much I was focusing on my health issues, maybe because he believed the more I thought about them, the worse they would get.

A week later, I made the trip on my own to Whitehorse for the blood work per the clinic doctor's requisition. I decided to take advantage of the cell service and had a session with my life coach, whom I had started seeing back in Dawson to help me navigate the challenges I was experiencing. I had been attending sessions with her for around six months. With the pressures I'd been faced with at work, my pending decision to leave the position of Land and Resources Manager, internal conflicts I'd been experiencing, and my mounting physical symptoms, I'd at least had the wherewithal to reach out to someone "professional" I could talk to about what was going on. While Jeremy did his best to support me, I knew I needed another listening ear to help me figure out some things in my life.

Besides, some of the issues I needed to process ran deeper, like abusive relationships and my childhood, and I couldn't expect Jeremy to work through these with me in the dedicated way that was required. After a nerve-wracking wait for my blood test results, they all came back showing my blood levels within normal ranges and, most importantly, negative for lupus. Although I was relieved to know I hadn't tested positive for an autoimmune disease, at the same time, I felt uneasy not knowing what was going on with my body. I tried to take some pleasure in the simple gardening life of weeding, meditating, and walking our three dogs, but the ever-pressing unknown continued to haunt me. I smeared bottled aloe across my burning hands, tongued the small, clear sores newly developing along the insides of my mouth, and fed my worries with Google searches of every possible ailment I could have, on our spotty, satellite internet.

Although I was highly distracted by my health concerns, I still created a day-to-day routine for myself to cultivate a sense of solace, no matter how unimportant my days on the farm felt compared with my former work in Dawson. I truly wanted to adjust to the nurturance of my new surroundings and make the most of the break, but as I opened up to the potential of healing, I was instead greeted by a large, empty space in my psyche; I felt alone and disconnected, even with Jeremy around. *Have I lost my way, or worse yet, myself?*

In the mornings before Jeremy woke up, I would quietly slide around him on our double bed in my small travel camper before slipping out the door and walking to the older, larger camper that served as our kitchen 10 metres away. A few weeks after our arrival at the property, the cold, thick morning air still held fast in the galley, and I could see my breath even though it was June. I brushed mice feces off the counter one particular morning and shuddered at the mangled corpse in the trap by the sink. "Ah, nothing like the joys of camp life to get a girl going in the morning." Saved by the gurgle of the percolator, I hastily poured myself a cup of strong, black coffee and added a couple lumps of sugar and a dash of milk. The old camper door closed with a clap behind me as I made for the lookout.

I spied the large, plastic lawn chair perched at the crest of the steep hill overlooking the garden and the O'Donnell River below. The chair looked out of place with its rigid, angular arms jetting out towards a backdrop of clear, briskly flowing water, untouched forests and pristine mountains. Its weathered blue frame made a sharp cracking noise as I sat down, and as I leaned back, I wondered, despite my slender build, whether it would hold me. I steadied myself and with both hands clutched the tin mug of hot coffee. My constantly cold hands were desperate for its heat, but instead of offering me a nurturing warmth, the hot dark liquid bit through the thin metal at my frigid palms and fingers. Apologetically, steam rose up from the scalding cup and gently caressed my cheeks, like a regretful mother. I set the cup upon the ground at my feet and reached into my vest pocket to pull out a small, grey notebook the size of my palm. Flipping through the pages, I stopped at the notes scribbled down from my last life coaching session I had over the phone in Whitehorse. My handwriting was scrawled across the paper as if in a desperate hurry to get somewhere. "Confused, lost, disconnected, HELP!" As I read what I had written, in addition to my overwhelming emotions, I recalled how curious I had been, both during the conversation and when I was reflecting on it immediately afterwards.

During our call, I expressed my desire to reach some kind of clarity and confidence within myself. "I so badly want to connect with my inner knowing. I want to find my own way."

My coach's voice was calm on the other end of the phone. She responded clearly and concisely, as if she were fully anticipating me to reach this internal inquiry at this exact time. I could hear her voice in my head as I traced my finger under the words on the page that captured her response that day. "Try asking the question, what do I know that I didn't know I already knew?"

I remembered how confused I felt when she had presented this idea for me to experiment with.

"So . . .," I said, shifting the receiver from one hand and ear to the other, before reflecting back to her: "Ask the question and wait for a response?"

"Yes."

"But who am I asking?"

It was her turn to pause. ". . . You . . . in a way," she replied, as if in invitation. "And what if I don't respond?" I was quick to retort since the whole thing seemed a bit strange to me.

"It's interesting, isn't it, Kay?"

"How can I know something I didn't know I knew? And If I do, how come I've been keeping that from myself?"

"Well, it might take some time and if you keep opening and allowing, she—the one who knows—will come around, maybe in an unexpected way or from a surprising place."

I put the notebook back in the vest pocket, picked up the gleaming cup beside me, and took a sip of the now-slightly-cooler coffee. "Well, here goes nothing."

I placed the cup down on the wide armrest and pulled my still cold hands under the long sleeves of my sweater. As I sank back into the chair, I exhaled deeply and closed my eyes. The chickadees and warblers sang with increasing vitality as the sun gained presence in the morning's sky.

Alongside the birds' chorus, I recited, "What do I know that I didn't know I already knew?"

With purposeful breaths, in and out, I attempted to remember. I sat quietly for some time, but there was no reply. Diligently, I expanded my question outward to the wild animals in the surrounding bush. I imagined my question floating out on the breeze and reverberating on the ear hair of a foraging bear. Could he hear me? Still no reply. So I expanded my question further to the trees. The aspen leaves chattered in the wind as if in response, but I could not understand their language. The harder I tried and the more I attempted to focus my breath, the less connected I felt. As my frustration built, the wind died down and the leaves stopped rustling. Then I asked again. This time, I was met with an ultimate silence. I could no longer hear the chorus of chickadees and warblers.

The hard, plastic surface of the chair dug into my seat bones and I wormed around its unforgiving breadth as if trying to escape my uncomfortable skeleton. *I need out. I need out of this fucking body.* I felt completely closed off to my surroundings and extremely vulnerable. A pain surfaced through the left side of my rib cage and my left shoulder twitched in a sticky discomfort. A loud gurgling noise shot out of my stomach in protest and I felt a strangling sensation in my throat. My tongue throbbed in a bath of deep-seated anxiety and my teeth clenched tightly against each other as if trying to break their way free. *A frail, uncertain, raging body, is that all there is? Has it always felt this way?*

A memory from my childhood came rushing in.

I was standing in a heavy downpour on the streets of the neighbourhood where I grew up. My arms were outstretched in complete invitation of the pelting rain. I was soaked and stood shoeless. My socked feet were submerged under the rippling surface of a massive puddle, and water wormed between my toes. Closing my eyes, I craned my neck backwards, showing my beaming face to the sky. There was a familiar power up there who recognized my smile, and with some kind of magic, she washed away the uncertain.

"What do I know that I didn't know I already knew?" The coach's voice merged with mine in that moment as I repeated the question out loud, allowing the childhood memory to return to the place where memories live. I noticed my ribcage felt a little freer; my stomach settled slightly and I was able to relax my jaw. As I gazed up at the pale blue sky, a slight smile crept to my eyes. Where it would go from there was anybody's guess.

In the afternoons, I regularly walked the dogs down to Atlin Lake to spend time by the open water. It only took about twenty minutes to arrive at the lake's shore, where the O'Donnell River emptied into its vast expanse. Once on the beach, we would watch the terns. They would fly directly toward us as if delivering a message and once they reached us, they would stop in mid-air and flap stationary above our heads. One day I brought a sketch-book and drew the tern in sight above me. Then I added the dogs and the head and right shoulder of a black bear I imagined surveying us from the cover of the forest. I drew the tern's sight lines to reveal how the bird was viewing me and the dogs, and then I drew the bear's sight lines, which included us all. I wanted to capture the feeling of being watched by the wild.

Every day, I would follow the same trail to the beach, a path lined with spruce, cottonwood, willow and balsam fir. I marvelled at the balsam fir trees, which felt novel to me as I had never seen them grow in the Yukon. Their bark was smooth and silver, reminiscent of young salmon, and lined with pitch pockets of healing sap. I collected the oily sap by piercing the sacks with my buck knife and cupping the sticky juice into small, plastic containers. Then I mailed it up to my friend, an Elder in Dawson, who used it as a key ingredient in various medicines. Following her example, I even tried it as remedy on my hand sores, unfortunately with little relief.

One day while making my way along the trail to the lake, I bumped into two young men. It was an event to see anyone else walking in the area. One of the guys was tall with blond hair and blue eyes. The other was shorter with a stocky build, dark brown hair and brown eyes. They introduced themselves as Burt and Andy.

I beamed at them, excited to meet others along my usually solo afternoon jaunt.

"Where you headed?"

Andy's eyes sparkled in return as if in acknowledgment of a fellow adventurer. "We're back-packing to Telegraph Creek!"

"The trail is super overgrown because it was built in the early 1900s," Burt said, "but we are trying to find it." He looked down to re-adjust his back-pack straps then back up at me.

"It's over 250 kilometres if we make it all the way to the small town of Telegraph," said Andy, peering down at his feet. He shuffled them in the leaf litter as if to warm them up for the trek ahead.

"Wow, I wish you guys the best adventure! I would love to hear how it went when you get back to town." I smiled at the two travellers one last time and called our dogs back from the bush.

My stomach still fluttered with excitement as I walked back to the farm later that afternoon. Jeremy was busy breaking up a new garden bed with his back-hoe, so I waved at him to turn the thrumming engine off. I pulled myself up the first step of the large, yellow machine and looked up at him in the cab. With enthusiasm, I told him about the travellers I had just met.

"Oh yeah? That's something, eh. Quite the undertaking."

"Right?!? So cool, eh."

The afternoon's sunlight flashed in the blue of his eyes. "Well, it sure sounds like something. I wonder if they'll make it?"

"Yeah, I wonder. Sounds like the trail is super overgrown."

"I bet it is. I don't think anyone has hiked it in years."

"Yeah, maybe a bit crazy, but don't you think it's kind of exciting? To just up and go like that."

Jeremy smiled at me and turned the key to start the engine back up. "Nothing short of an adventure, Babe, and by the look on your face that might be just what you need." His voice was buoyant and loud overtop of the growling back-hoe.

Later that evening, we shared stories of adventures we had taken years before meeting each other. I looked over at Jeremy while changing into warmer sleeping clothes on the bed. "I really enjoyed the short canoe trips Andrea and I used to do on the Slocan." Located in south-eastern BC, that lake was kitty-corner to where Jeremy and I were now, near Atlin Lake, at the far north-west corner of the province. I remembered my friend Andrea and I paddling along the serene, slender body of inviting water. We gazed at the tawny pictographs protected by rock overhangs along the western shore, the deeply imbedded presence of the Sinixt First Nation who travelled this waterway well before the Kootenay's "silver rush" of the late 1800s.

Jeremy sat down on the sofa, peeled off his socks, and placed them on the cushion top behind him. "Oh man, I did the Dyea to Dawson race with Roger back in the 90s . . . that was epic! Years before that, I did that same trip, but solo, from the Chilkoot Trail back to Dawson. I also did some white-water kayaking trips in Ontario when I was a young buck."

"So cool, Babe." I could envision a much younger Jeremy out on the rivers in pursuit of adventure, with a wide-mouthed grin and lit up eyes. He was confidently forging through the wild, unpredictable waters with his strong physique. Always pushing himself to live in a larger-than-life way, after his battle with Crohn's Disease, he made an incredible recovery and never looked back. He would tell me how it was all borrowed time.

"You know," Jeremy piped up again, "it's so interesting to think that back in the day people used to use these waterways like highways."

"Oh, so true, eh." I remembered seeing black and white photographs of the Tr'ondëk Hwëch'in in their birch bark canoes on the Yukon River in the board room where I used to attend meetings. And the wreckage of the massive steam powered boats from the Gold Rush era, their remains slowly disintegrating back into the earth in the paddlewheel graveyard just downriver from Dawson. "I bet the lakes and rivers have a story or two to tell of those times. It would be so cool to see people getting back out there and doing journeys on the same routes. Kinda like a pilgrimage!"

Jeremy listened to me intently, then bent over to put on his camp slippers. As he sat back up, he looked over at me flashing his whites. "Wow. I just had a thought."

I returned his gaze with a silly grin. "What? Did it hurt?"

"Kinda!" He snickered. "I just realized that the waterways from Atlin all the way north to Dawson are completely connected!" He leaned into the small table with the look of an idea on his face and started to rub the back of his laptop with the palm of his hand.

I turned my body to face him and uncrossed my legs. "That's so cool! Wouldn't it be amazing to do a paddling trip from here back to Dawson?"

"One sec!" he said, before bolting upright and out of the camper.

I could hear him pulling the cord on the small generator outside and it started to hum. The camper lights flickered on and Jeremy re-entered. He sat down at the table and powered up the laptop.

"Let's check the route out on Google Maps."

I joined him on the sofa and peered over his shoulder at the laptop screen. He clicked the cursor starting at the O'Donnell River near our garden and onward through a chain of lakes and rivers that ended in Dawson City. We estimated the trip to be just under 1000 kilometres long.

"Hmm. Kayaks might be the best bet," Jeremy said, closing the laptop. "They carry more gear and are safer and easier than canoes in rough water and weather."

I ran my fingers through my tangled hair as a smile lit up my face. "I've always really liked kayaks . . . though I've only been in one once!"

He placed his hand on my head and tousled my hair back into a mess. "We would need big ones like those long sea kayaks."

I grabbed his hand off my head, moved closer to him on the sofa, and put my forehead to his, staring directly into his eyes. "It'd be awesome to try out sea kayaks," I said, before my lips found his through his overgrown facial hair. A gentle kiss sealed the idea.

Connected Waterways

I was the one who made the definitive decision to do the trip; Jeremy was there to support me as far as he could go. I scheduled it for the end of August and set aside two weeks to complete it. My job interview in Dawson was set in September, so I had limited time to complete the journey.

After much internal debate and discussion with my former supervisor, I had determined it would be best for me to leave my former role as Land and Resources Manager and apply for a different position working for the same First Nation. I felt the new position could be a better fit for me and remembered enjoying working with its direct supervisor in the past.

Before the decision, I was very unsure about what I was going to do after the summer. Our time gardening in Atlin was naturally coming to a close and we would be moving back to Dawson in September to spend the winter there. I knew I would need to start working again; I needed the money and no other options were calling to me. After months of gardening and being with the land at the farm and reconnecting with my creativity by sketching wildlife at the beach, I felt tentatively ready for re-entry into the work-world, and was antsy to at least try. So, after I saw the new position posted, I applied and soon after was awarded an interview. I really had no idea how long the trip would take, so I felt nervous about our arbitrary timeline. I hoped the two-week timeframe we came up with would be doable somehow.

The other wrinkle in our plans was that it turned out Jeremy was not going to be able to join me for the full length of the journey back to Dawson; we realized this shortly after I scheduled the trip. This meant I'd be travelling a great distance and most of the allotted time solo. Jeremy seemed somewhat uncomfortable with the idea of me being out there in the wilderness alone on remote waterways. His main concerns were my lack of kayaking experience and limited practice making tough decisions under physical and mental duress when out there alone in the elements. He was worried that on my own, I may find the journey too tough, and if so, what would I do? I could get stranded out there with limited access to help for getting me to safety. Even with his worries, and my own nerves about the extent of the solo undertaking, I assured him the choice was mine to make and that I wanted to do the trip, even if a large part of it would be by myself. With everything I'd been through in Dawson before taking the time away at the farm and surrounding wilderness outside of Atlin, the journey felt important to me. In some ways, my willingness to undertake the long paddle on unfamiliar waters was made out of compulsion. There was something I was seeking, or there was something seeking me. I had to find out what. True to my nature to date, I was not dissuaded by the promise of difficulty. Jeremy knew the stubbornness of my character well, so was attuned to the fact that once I made an impassioned decision, I wouldn't be changing my mind. He must have figured the next best option was to at least get me as ready as possible for the epic adventure ahead.

That very week, we purchased two, seventeen-foot-long sea kayaks, which were on sale in Kelowna, BC and got them shipped to Whitehorse. A couple of weeks later, we picked up our shiny new boats and hauled them back to the farm. We decided to start with a test paddle on the O'Donnell River downstream to Atlin Lake. As we walked down to the river with our kayaks, its water chattered gleefully up at us as it washed over rounded stones and swept against sloughing banks. *Huh. Interesting. I never noticed how lively you were until now.*

During the test run, we came across a large dam of trees, only a few bends downstream from the farm. Jumbled across the entire width of the river, the log jam looked like a giant game of pick-up sticks. We successfully practiced pulling ashore and portaging to avoid the entrapment. By the end of our mini-trip, I had named my kayak Sugar Snap, for its bright green colour, and Jeremy's Hawkweed, for its bright yellow hue.

We then stocked up on all the food and gear we would need: dried meals, bush-kitchen supplies, mini-cook stove, tent, sleeping foamy, rain gear, extra clothes, bear bangers, bear spray, throw rope, tarp. We borrowed an inReach from Jeremy's friend Phillipe so that we could do safety check-ins. It provided a GPS tracking system and satellite connection for text messages so that others could keep track of my location. I also packed my solar charger for my cell phone. I added a map book to the pile, which included the Yukon River north of Carmacks to Dawson City. The first stretch of the river and the connected trail of lakes before that seemed like a straight shot, so we felt no reason to bring maps for those sections of the trip.

The day before our launch we packed our kayaks. I sat next to Sugar Snap completely surrounded by piles of food and gear. "How are we going to pack all of this stuff into our kayaks?" I mumbled to myself. Try after try, I couldn't figure out how to piece the puzzle together. Two hours in and I was still arranging and rearranging.

Jeremy walked over from his fully packed boat and peered down at me surrounded by all the gear. "We'll never get on the water at this rate!"

With his help, I was finally able to cram the chaos next to me into Sugar Snap. He was more comfortable with packing the boats as best we could for now, knowing that we would get lots of practice during our long journey. We each reached over to our respective vessels, and the fully loaded kayaks were almost too heavy for us to lift. Wisely, we had purchased a set of wheels we could use to tow the full boats to the river in the morning.

Once the kayaks were ready, the trip began to feel more real. I felt both excited and anxious about the undertaking, and was much more worked up about it than Jeremy for many reasons. The timeline would be tight, as I had the job interview in Dawson to make; that was important to me. I was also still contending with my mysterious, ongoing health concerns, which I suspected would get further aggravated from the stress of the trip. And, not only did I lack experience kayaking and camping in the backcountry, I would also be doing a large portion of the trip on my own. With Jeremy only able to join me on the journey as far as Whitehorse, that is, for the first 300 kilometres, I would be navigating the remaining 700 kilometres of the journey solo. This would mean at least eight days and nights by myself in the deep wilderness, across Lake Laberge and a lengthy stretch of the Yukon River back to Dawson. Even though I was excited for and had willingly accepted the upcoming adventure knowing that I would do much of it on my own, to say the solo portion of my upcoming travels was a bit of a daunting prospect is an understatement at best. Also, because I'd told many of my friends and my sisters about the trip, organized a fundraiser based on my successful arrival into Dawson for a First Nation leadership initiative that was dear to me, and even had a pre-trip radio interview to promote that fundraiser, I felt a good deal of pressure to complete the journey. Now, the question was, would I?

That night, Jeremy went out to visit with our closest neighbours about a kilometre down the road. Without cell service where we were, there was no way of communicating, and when he still wasn't home after 11, I fretted until his return at 2 am. By then, I was furious.

I peered over at his dark silhouette as he stumbled into the camper and towards the bed. "How could you be so carefree when we have this huge trip tomorrow?"

"Whoa, Babe, no need to get pissed. We'll see what the weather brings tomorrow morning. I heard it's gonna be windy." He fumbled into bed beside me.

"Come on, Jeremy, you know how important this trip is to me. A little wind isn't going to stop me." I squirmed as he fished under the covers and tried to put his arm around my waist.

"Kay, you know if there's wind on that lake, it can kick up real bad. The waves can even beach motor boats let alone flimsy little kayaks." His breath wafted across my cheek in a lightly scented breeze of peach schnapps.

"You stink." I wriggled as far out of his reach as I could on the small mattress and lay there rigid in anger, as if he could control the weather.

Although Jeremy and I shared a lot of love, our relationship had its challenges. I grew frustrated towards his chill attitude about the things that mattered most to me, like how he came home drunk the night before an early start to our big trip. And a wedge was developing between us due to my tenuous mental and physical states. I was more nervous than ever about what was going on with my body and in no mood for affection. I wished I was easier for him, or that our dynamic was easier sometimes, but it was a ridiculous prayer, like wishing a bee were a flower. It seemed like every circumstance we found ourselves in was testing us, to see whether our bond was strong enough to keep us together. During the dark, frigid months of the winter, after I told him that I didn't have space for him anymore, we split for a short while and then argued our way back together. For some reason, we were continually drawn to each other, even when we had rationalized ourselves apart. *But now, maybe now, this trip will be enough to finally separate us?* I ruminated on this very possible and unsettling future as I drifted off to sleep.

We woke up the next morning to tree tops swaying as birds flitted about in all directions across the light blue sky. Although we were both tired from the late night, adrenaline was coursing through my veins come daybreak, and I convinced Jeremy to get up early. In my mind, this trip was happening, wind or not, us being tired or not.

"Why did you put so much pressure on yourself for this trip?" Jeremy rubbed his eyes and blinked trying to adjust to the morning's light.

"What do you mean?"

"Well, instead of just going for a paddle, you had to tell all your friends, do a fundraiser, and even a radio interview."

"Well, it's just that I know it's going to be hard out there."

"Yeah, but, so?"

"I need the pressure so that I don't give up. So that if things get tough and I want to give up, I'll remember all the people counting on me and expecting me to finish the trip. Then it'll be harder to stop."

"Okay, I guess I get it. I just don't know why you always put so much pressure on yourself."

"Well, someone has to or else I wouldn't do anything."

We finished off some porridge for breakfast and I chugged a couple of strong coffees. The kayaks, still packed from the day before, were ready to tow down to the water's edge, except for one last thing.

I took the broach my friend Natasha had given me that was symbolic of my dog Mya. Mya had been killed the summer before by a hit and run on the highway leaving Dawson, a month before I had met Jeremy. The timing of Mya's death and meeting Jeremy was not lost on me. In a way, I felt like her leaving made room for me to open up and meet someone new, because with her I felt totally complete. The sudden loss of her left me feeling like a dismantled puzzle scattered across the margins of my life. She had been very much a part of my identity, so her departure left me confused as to who I was; who was left behind? Mya was like a soul mate to me, so it seemed fitting that her spirit would be my guardian on this long journey. I pinned the broach of the Siberian husky to the bow of Sugar Snap and imagined Mya was with me.

Our bond is endless. It snaps back into place when you let it be. I followed your trail, its meanderings. There is no need to feel lost. Only a need to ask. Forgive me for my departure. It was ripe with darkness. Your despair cracked open the heavens so that I could bound into my new life. Your heart crumbled the graces so that you would begin to ask. To ask how to connect back to the worlds you belong to. It's in these deep fissures and breakages that you find a way through. A way through to the worlds of your origin.

Complete with lucky figurehead secured, we loaded my kayak onto the tow wheels. Jeremy pulled her through the bumpy yard, down the slope, and alongside the garden to the grassy bank of the O'Donnell River. Then he circled back with the wheels, loaded up Hawkweed, and brought him down to the river as well. We pushed Sugar Snap's hull into the rushing water, and holding her bow upstream Jeremy stabilized the vessel as I entered the cockpit. Once I was safely in the kayak, he waded over to Hawkweed, pulled him into the water and ferried him across to the opposite bank where it was shallower. As he entered his kayak, I paddled against the current to slow myself from floating too far downstream. Hawkweed quickly caught up and the river took us. Within moments, we had lost sight of the farm and were being pulled around a sharp bend. Having paddled the river during our test run, we anticipated the log jam well in advance and aimed for a rocky beach just up-river from it. We helped each other portage our heavy kayaks across the gravel and entered back into the river downstream of the jumbled crisscross of timber.

The morning was bright and sunny, and despite the strong wind, it was a beautiful start to our journey. We floated by the large, half submerged spruce tree, which we had affectionately named the "boat launch" after using it as a kind of dock for Jeremy's small motor boat during high water, then past a network of deeply imbedded beaver trails along the river's edge. They were worn and stripped of vegetation from all of the large rodents' comings and goings into and out of the water. The current slowed and the river straightened and widened. It was about 15 metres from shore to shore now and the banks were covered in heavily browsed willow. This transition of the river and landscape, signalled we were nearing the outlet into Atlin Lake. Jeremy looked over at me and smiled as we paddled side-by-side. "It's really cool we're doing this Kay. Here we are, starting a new story. I'm so glad we're doing this part together."

Jeremy's comment warmed my heart and helped me forgive him a little for the night before. "It's super exciting, and I'm glad you're here with me too, especially for the massive lakes." I smiled back and the energy between us softened.

Ahead of us in the late morning's light, a flock of Canada geese was also paddling towards the open water. In a procession, the assured wildfowl led us to deeper water in a series of honks.

As we hit the "mixing zone" where the river entered the lake, we paddled straight out to avoid the riotous waves crashing up against the beach. The wind was strong and even though we were trying to avoid them by steering north and staying far enough away from the shore to evadethe breakwater, the waves still swelled and crashed over the hulls of our kayaks. Within minutes, my hands were soaked and the frigid water was running up my jacket sleeves and seeping intrusively under my loose-fitting top and down to the lower part of my torso, shocking my tender skin. Even with my water-resistant spray skirt snuggly cinched around my chest, the unrelenting water had found its way in. A feeling of failure set into my bones. I looked over at Jeremy to see how he was coping with the less-than-ideal conditions. But instead of seeing a struggling paddler, Jeremy was smiling and paddling gracefully with the unsettling waves. The deep turquoise water contrasted sharply with the vibrant yellow of Hawkweed. The scene was spectacular: wide open azure waters against majestic, white capped mountains. The waves were so high that at times Jeremy's kayak was obscured from view, leaving his upper body and head magically afloat on the distending surface. Even still, Jeremy had a relaxed air about him like he was in his element, like he was at home in the water. It reminded me of his Piscean astrology. *The fish has found his water.*

The last time I saw you, you were dancing out loud. You were playing and laughing, you made my heart sing. I saw that you didn't want me. That you were unsure and that made my heart cry. Will we be as one? Or part ways through these waves of life? I admired your love for the unknown, I seek it too. I admired the way you crumbled and crashed into your life, like you had nothing to lose. Now I feel like the loser. Someone who could lose it all through the thrashing of your tail and the white caps of your Kali. In life, death, and life, I will be reborn to you. I will be in love with you and hold your hand like it is the most precious thing. I may believe your warmth even though cold water is all that really seeps in. Express yourself, but don't leave me cold. Come warm me up and keep me afloat of my life. I'm sorry that I tremble in your strength. I could nonetheless hold you close while you tear into my heart. You tell me it's because you want to love me. Is it because you want to know me? I don't know. I don't know. Your spirit is wild, and that is why I love you. My spirit is wild and that is why you struggle, but I know you love me for who I truly am. Maybe we are both afraid of each other's wild? Like it might come at us and we won't know what to do with it. Let it in? Or put up our arms up in a posture as if to say "I don't want any trouble."

We had been on the lake for about an hour and the wind continued to gain strength. My heart pounded as the waves broke all around us in white layers of foam and searing rushes.

"Jeremy!"

"Yeah?"

"Let's head for shore! It's getting too rough out here." As I spoke, an unexpected wave furled and spat up across my skirt and along my lower back.

Our first day on this extremely long journey was a complete flop. We wouldn't make any distance today unless the wind calmed down. We scanned the shoreline for a safe place to pull over. Soon, we saw a gravel bar and the outlet of a small creek with milky water.

Jeremy steered towards the landmark. "Let's head for that creek ahead."

I could barely hear him over the waves. "Okay! Is that McKee?"

"I think so."

We knew McKee Creek well because we drove over it regularly on our way from Atlin to the farm. From the bridge, about two kilometres inland of the lake's eastern shoreline, you could see an active placer mine scouring the creek's bed for gold. We paddled hard, rushing our kayaks into the creek's cloudy mouth. Once we were well-protected in the outlet, we eagerly emerged from our kayaks and pulled them onto the gravel bar. We looked back at the boisterous lake. White caps flickered across its surface, an active expression of the incessant wind. The methodical crashing of the break water on the gravel was relentless.

Jeremy rubbed his eyes and wiped his face as if to shed an old layer. "Well, that was a rough start."

I exhaled in an overly dramatic sigh.

Jeremy patted me on the back. "Ah well. Let's set up our tent to get out of the wind."

It was only noon but I was tired of being exposed to the gale force winds. "Fine."

We struggled to put the tent up in the persistent wind and each took turns holding it down while the other erected the tent poles and hammered tent pegs. Once we had the billowing tent secured and our beds made, Jeremy immediately laid down. He was still fatigued from the night before. I was able to get him to play a few games of squiggle and hangman before he turned over and fell asleep. I picked up my book *A Return to Love,* by Marianne Williamson, and tried to focus on its heart-felt lessons rather than obsess over my disappointment with our lack of miles and Jeremy's lack of enthusiasm. I felt bummed that Jeremy wasn't as committed to this trip as I was, even though it was my idea to see it through. Later, after Jeremy roused from his nap, we ventured outside the tent and started searching for unique stones along the beach. Jeremy loved rock collecting, and decided to start a collection. I liked the idea, so started looking for special stones to contribute. I brought a handful of my finest to him for final judgment, and though most of them didn't make the cut, he accepted a few of the brightest coloured ones and added them to the pile of loose stones on the floor of his kayak's cockpit. Then, we shared a dinner of beans and hot chocolate, but neither of us spoke much. The food soothed my deflated mood with a temporary sugar fix, but the feeling of failure quickly returned. *We have to make up miles tomorrow*, I told myself, as I drifted off into a restless sleep next to Jeremy, who was dead to the world.

Underneath where the water churns, I dance my love away. I could believe you were there, but you are not. I don't see you, only shadows of your promise above. When will you come around to seeing the dance I am in? The dance of sacrifice and faith. A dance so involved and delicate that at any minute it could crack open and let the ocean in. I am swift yes, wild and curious, delightful, playful and in awe of life. But I am also swimming in the muck of it, in the thickest current and deepest undertow. Do you believe me when I say "I love you?" Or do you believe me more when I say "this hurts?" I have been asking myself for a year about the importance of our love and I can come up with only one thing. I have faith in our love. I don't know if that answers my quest, but it gives me something to hold onto. A life-line between me and you. I still have these dreams you know, it doesn't make them disappear, it actually makes them stay, as if realized in some kind of possibility or dimension. Alive to me still as a potential. Alive to me still as gifts of an outer world, promises of perpetual life.

I opened my eyes to the early morning's light and my ears scanned for the sound of waves: silence. *Good news*, I thought, *the wind has died down.*

Jeremy and I emerged from the tent and cooked up some oatmeal. In a rush to catch the good weather, we pulled down and packed our tent, played Tetris placing our gear back into the kayaks, and started out early onto the calm water. We continued our way north along the eastern shore of Atlin Lake.

Not long after we started paddling, nature called.

"Hey, Babe?"

"Yeah?"

"I gotta go."

"Yeah, me too." "Let's stop there." Jeremy pointed at a broad beach in a bay tucked away from the open water.

I followed him and we beached with a sound like sandpaper refining the underside of our boats. Atlin townsite was directly north and within sight of the protected cove. The beach and surrounding area looked well used by roadside pit-stoppers. There were candy wrappers and empties on the beach, and when I walked into the bush to find some privacy, I noticed toilet paper strewn throughout the grass and willow shrubs. Further along a sandy path, I caught a glimpse of a bright white skull and spine from a small canine. On either side of me stood stunted aspen trees with sparse, gnarly limbs twisting in great efforts toward the sky.

I was suddenly transported back to an afternoon two weeks prior. I had picked up a woman hitchhiking home to the reservation.

"He drank a 40-pounder of vodka and hung himself from a tree near the water," she said, as she pointed out my truck window towards the shoreline. "Some German tourists found him hanging there while they were out for a walk."

I closed my eyes for a moment to shake the image.

Back at the kayaks, I put my spray skirt on and zipped up my lifejacket to prepare for launch. Jeremy looked over at me with concern. "You okay, Hun?"

"Oh yeah, why?"

"You look pale."

"Oh, it's nothing."

"Umm, okay . . ."

I squished the unsettled feeling down into my stomach and slipped into my kayak's seat. Without further question, Jeremy launched me backwards into the shallow water of the bay with a valiant push. Facing shore, I silently bobbed in the shallows. As I waited for him, I remembered what an Elder from Dawson said to me before I left for Atlin.

"Dear, why are you going to Atlin when that community is in so much pain?"

I hadn't fully understood what she meant until the woman hitchhiking had shared her story with me. I was also aware that the effects of colonization and inter-generational trauma from residential school wasn't isolated to specific communities; it was wide-spread. Back in Dawson, I knew many First Nation people who struggled from its plundering destruction. I witnessed them battle daily with their addictions, which they used to numb the pain, and some of the, young, bright, intelligent, and creative souls, would be pushed to the point of losing their own lives. Each life lost would send unbearable waves of grief through the First Nation and larger community. The streets of Dawson would lose their lustre and the liveliness of the community faded as yet one more unique star frayed into the blackness of the winter night's sky.

After working for the Tr'ondëk Hwëch'in in Dawson, I also came to learn of their enduring strength and resilience that had brought them through some of the most unbelievable atrocities and sadness; the strength to re-build and recreate their culture from collapse and their generosity and forgiveness, which I received from many as they brought me in and shared their wisdom.

"Let's cross the lake here." I looked back at Jeremy before paddling into the deeper water. I didn't want to risk the temptation of stopping in town and calling it quits.

"Okay, well, it's a narrower crossing up ahead across from town, but I get it." Jeremy followed supportively.

We paddled diagonally across the lake from the bay and avoided Atlin altogether. The wind was in our favour, and it gently pushed us along in remorseful pulses as if apologetic for the blustery day before. Once we reached the other side of the massive lake, I began to relax. Away from town, I started to feel like we were going to pull this trip off.

In a silent gesture, Atlin slowly faded from beside us to behind us. We hugged the western shore and chose a course between a series of small islands. Pausing our paddles, we drifted for a few moments, absorbing their rugged faces and weathered trees. Flocks of chatty gulls circled a pock of land disturbing a bald eagle from her nest.

Our time on Atlin Lake was coming to a close. Soon we would be paddling Atlin River, a portal into a tract of wilderness even further removed from people. The river emptied into Taku Arm, followed by Tagish Lake, both areas we had never explored before. With no communities until Tagish, we would be paddling in isolation for over 100 kilometres.

Before launching the trip, Jeremy and I had asked around to the locals about Atlin River. Very few people I spoke with had been on it, except for a couple of die-hard back-to-the-landers, or those who had ventured it in their youth, fifty decades prior. There was one local adventurer I spoke with who had paddled the river one early summer when the water was lower. She showed a map to me, which demarcated a short, narrow river, about five kilometres long, running in a north-westerly direction from the western shore of Atlin Lake, with many curves and numerous rocky outcrops. Arrows lightly etched on the map marked the best routes around obstructing boulders.

Jeremy gently glided further off shore, then looked over his left shoulder at me. "Umm, I think the river starts just up ahead."

"Okay. This'll be exciting." I seized my paddle tightly and put on a somewhat sarcastic, wide-mouthed grin.

We steered our kayaks closer to the shoreline so we wouldn't miss it. Suddenly, by an invisible force, the water pulled us to our left. All around us, the surface of the lake began to swirl.

Jeremy looked down at the activated water and then up at its destination. "Oh man. The whole of Atlin Lake is being sucked into this river!"

"This is crazy!" I looked straight ahead in anticipation.

I could see the voluminous water steering out of view around a treed bluff about 200 metres ahead.

Jeremy looked inland towards me. "Holy cow! You're moving fast!"

I glanced over at the shoreline and watched the trees flicker by as I whizzed past them at an increasing rate. "Whoa, I totally am." I looked back at Jeremy wide-eyed.

A loon, floating just out of reach of the current, called dramatically at us.

Out there is where you will be. Make it away from yourself. West into the waters of my dwelling. You will find there a treasure of proportions beyond gold, beyond the striking nature of the rich.

Fledglings holler, but they don't know the reason. They holler because of the wind. The wind hollers back. We call to each other. "Where are you?" "I am over here." A game, a trance of song, a deciphering of the code. Where will I find you, young fledgling? And where are you going? Those waters break the dead and cough up the dying. Will you be one of them? The lost souls trapped beneath the surface of bubbling atrocities. Or will you find grace in the unknown beneath your carriage? I wish you well. We wish you well. Above and below worlds of recognition.

If it suits you, I will rest here on these calm waters of reflection. I know your journey, as I know my own. One of birth, life, and death, though I'm not quite ready. Forgive my patience, but I must sit as you wander. I must hold fast as you seek, so that you may find the journey worthy, so that you may leave and so that I may return to drift upon these waters. May you be protected and unleashed from your shackles. May you be loved and unloved all the same. May you lose your way so that you can find your wreckage and pray the pieces back together again. It's okay to be wounded and wander all the same. It's okay to be lost and wander all the same.

Where would this slim river take me? What could I leave behind? What lay ahead to be gained? Our time at the farm was coming to an end, I had the job interview to attend back in Dawson, and my leave of absence from my current position had given me time to reflect, and to rest. What had I learned? What good had come? And how would things be now between Jeremy and me? Questions and feelings churned and mingled within even as the rapid current took me.

I glanced over at the wise bird, who was mirrored by the safe, glassy water beneath her, then looked at Jeremy.

Hawkweed was being pulled closer to Sugar Snap by the current and Jeremy looked uneasy. "Well, it looks like we don't have the choice to turn back now." Our boats careened closer together then parallel to one another.

As the current pulled us around the bluff, the inlet of the river came into view. I gripped my paddle with clenched fists, bracing myself for what was to come. The current increased to an even more dramatic speed, with the lake and river's water level at their peak of late August. Instead of visible boulders, rolling rapids stood as reminders of the outcrops beneath the water's surface. The forested river banks quickly morphed into steep, sloughing walls of sand and rock and the river narrowed dramatically. We were funneled into its slim span and had very few maneuvering options. As we came around the first bend, a strong eddy swept Jeremy's kayak up against the steep rocky bank, and spun him back to front.

I passed him while he was facing upstream and he looked over at me with a mixed expression of horror and excitement. "You okay?"

"Couldn't be better!" I smiled back at him with glee. The otherworldly river had called me out of my mind and into the moment.

There you are in the middle of my water. Gasping for air, but you are not drowning, you are simply learning how to breathe.

There you are, swirling amidst my up and down tows, I bring you where you want to be. I rush into your soul and lift you to heights before yourself. There you are, do you see?

So beautiful and raw. So unapologetically yourself. Unearthed and washed. There you are, exposed to the world.

After catching his breath, Jeremy stabbed his paddle back into the main current, and in a split second, it corrected his boat and led him back down the roiling water.

Over the thundering rage and froth, I looked over my shoulder at him. "Watch out for the big waves ahead!"

He managed to avoid them better than me. After little success, I decided to release my efforts of steering away from the tumbling monsters and instead charged my kayak straight through them. Cold water smashed against my chest kicking up spray onto my face and glasses so that I could barely see. The river narrowed again and the northeastern bank grew steeper still to match its neighbouring shore. It felt like being thread through the eye of a needle.

Shattering roars or raging frothy water plastering against my boulders and shores of resistance. Here I am! Look at me. Smell me. Hear me. Touch me. Taste me. Feel me. Here I am. My life is abundant and unapologetic. Here I am!

Can you see now how blessed you really are? I shout out your blessings up against the canyon walls.

At our pinnacle of overwhelm, we caught a glimpse of serene waters up ahead. It was the inlet of Taku Arm and our oasis. We would need to pass through the river's last, most gregarious wave, before reaching Taku Arm's sanctity. Jeremy was able to skirt left of the churning water, and I parted deeply through its right side. With me partially closing my eyes and holding my breath, Sugar Snap worked her magic. She plunged through the effervescent surf of the beastly swell. With her intelligent design, she wriggled and contorted out of the wave's embrace and onto the inviting riffles of shallower water. In a collective sigh of relief, we glided over the placid waters of the inlet, and immediately upon arrival, I erupted into euphoric laughter.

I am aliveness. I will never retire, only twist and turn and break and transform.

I hear the raging of your nature in my abdomen, like a thundering, sideways-slanting downpour pelting through my being.

We are together in this aliveness.

I felt a new appreciation of knowing I was alive after experiencing the river. Its very intensity had given me the gift of feeling present for the first time in years.

I felt enamoured with its unrelenting waters that broke through walls I had put up around my heart as some kind of protection against the world. I wasn't exactly sure when I began building them, probably during the family conflicts I endured as a child, but I knew the building of the walls hadn't stopped and the work had continued well into my adulthood and into my relationship with Jeremy. I imagined the walls were constructed with layers, brick, mortar, 2x4's, plywood, drywall and with extensive additions, to make sure there was as much space as possible between my heart and the outside world. The strength of the river's waves and the force of its current was what it took to topple these constructs so I could feel again. I was shocked to discover, once the walls came down, it wasn't fear that came crashing in, rather it was elation. Joy that I was alive. A genuine kind of happiness that felt fresh and care-free like the cascading laughter of a loved child. I wished I could stay in the pure excitement of the river so I could embody the presence he gave me forever.

Take me in. Wrap me up. Hold me close in your beating waves. Plaster me against your boulders and keep me there. Consume me in your churning waters. Don't let me escape. Keep me close so that I can better understand your ways, your bright hurting anger. I don't want to leave you, I only want to stay so that I can describe your life, your gestures, and your very way of being.

Graham Inlet, on the Taku Arm of Tagish Lake, accepted our successful passage of Atlin River with such a calm demeanour that it almost erased our adrenaline-filled experience of riding through the rapids. We paddled into a small cove at the south side of the Inlet and took refuge on its peaceful shore. My body trembled as I hoisted my kayak out of the water and flopped down onto the pebbled beach.

We were both breathing heavily and Jeremy turned to me with a smile of disbelief. "Wow, Babe, I couldn't believe you out there. You were smiling and almost laughing! And you handled the rapids like they were nothing!"

I took off my ball cap and wiped my forehead with my shirt sleeve. "Oh my God, that was something else. I did not expect that! I still can't believe it." I took a deep breath and gazed with contentment into Jeremy's sparkling, blue eyes. In that moment, I almost felt why he loved me.

In tranquil reprieve, we looked north across the Inlet at the old train station and cabins built during the gold rush era. A cow moose emerged from the cover of an island directly across from the cabins and waded into the water. The mid-afternoon's sunlight flickered off the inlet's surface haloing her silhouetted body as she made sure-footed movements into the depths. Then, the dark, smaller shape of her calf appeared on the island's shore near her. He took small, hesitant steps as he waded out to follow his mother. He stopped in the water about knee deep and patiently watched as she fed on weeds further out. Although he was young, the calf moose knew full well how much water he could handle. Even the youngest animals out here had a wisdom much greater than my own. I was humbled by this realization and grateful once again that the otherworldly river had allowed us safe passage. Its waters were certainly well beyond anything I had imagined or expected to handle.

Once we were fueled up with granola bars, dried fruit and chocolate, we entered our kayaks anew and began the venture west down the Taku Arm towards Tagish Lake. It was mid-afternoon and our goal was to arrive at the body of Tagish Lake before nightfall.

As soon as we paddled away from the shelter of the inlet, we were confronted by a headwind from the west. I followed Jeremy paddling close to the southern shore of the arm. The further we paddled, the stronger the wind got and before long it became a relentless wall.

Jeremy took the lead. "Hey, let's aim for that spit of land ahead. We can take a break from the wind there."

"Okay." As if bench-pressing, I pushed my paddle into the wind with all my might.

Unfortunately, we couldn't simply pull to the shore and walk our kayaks along the shoreline. The water was dreadfully cold and the shoreline was too rocky and overgrown. Stuck on the water, we were only able to maintain a walking pace, even with our greatest efforts. Jeremy read the water, finding paths of least resistance in the small trails of smooth surface along the shoreline. I did my best to follow, but my arms began to throb in pain and I could feel my shoulder muscles tearing. The pain was excruciating and dampened my spirits immensely as I knew I was already injuring my body at the onset of this massive journey. In addition to the pain, I was perplexed by how quickly things could shift out here on the water. I had recently felt euphoric after our successful navigation of Atlin River and now, just like that with a change of conditions, I felt defeated and consumed by pain. To try and keep my mind off the pain and to measure my progress, I chose a tree along the shoreline and watched it carefully. It remained steadfast beside me for ten minutes straight as I paddled with all I had. I was no longer moving forward. My throat ached in distress and tears welled in my eyes and began streaming down my face. The wind tugged at them and pulled their trickles across my cheeks and into my ears. I could not fathom overcoming this standstill.

The wind makes a sound so strong it blows my mind away. It dries me up and sets me adrift into a world of chaos and turmoil.

"Maybe we should pull over?"

Jeremy, was to my right now, and he turned towards me as he continued to paddle determinedly into the wind. "If we stop here, we won't make the trip."

"What do you mean? We can stop and wait out the wind. We aren't getting anywhere anyways." Part of me knew the wind would never really stop and we didn't have time to wait it out if it did. Jeremy needed to get back to Whitehorse within the next three days so if we lost a day or even half of one, it would blow his timeline. Longer on the water also meant consuming more of our food supply, which we packed according to our planned timeframe.

"There are going to be lots of experiences on this trip that will be hard. Even if we aren't going far, we are still moving. We need to gain even a little bit. If we stop now, the trip is done."

Jeremy's stern words struck me deeply and my chest tightened. In a mixture of anger and despair, I brought attention to the pain in my shoulders and somehow harnessed it to push forward. For the next hour, we paddled the kayaks at an extremely slow walk towards the spit of land.

To our right, a mottled craggy mountain came into sight. Its ridge of jagged, towering boulders changed form as we slowly moved down the arm. As we got closer, it took on the appearance of a wolf head with sharp, pointy ears. In its presence, I discovered a hypnotic rhythm that found me a way to push ahead.

I heard your face, sway in and sway out, telling me to keep going, telling me I had it in me to do this. I struggled hard and found our peace, shared in times of glory and times of despair. It was the last bit of grit I had that made me complete again.

Once in the wind-shadow of the spit, we paddled with greater ease to the rocky beach. Jeremy drove hard to beach first, then he hauled my kayak, with me in it, onto the shore. I rested inside my beached boat for some time as the adrenaline wept out of my system.

I was letting go of what I thought I was capable of.

I wasn't sure exactly how I had mustered the additional strength to keep going in the unbearable wind and searing pain. Yes, Jeremy's words had impacted me hard and sank me into a desperation that brought up a tenacity from deep within I never knew I had. And also, there was the wind. Its force was inescapable, visceral. It felt like the wind was blowing through me and between the atoms of my cells, almost like I was made up of the wind and used its very power to rise with it. It felt blurry, like we had swapped forms, and just as the wind empowered me, my spirit had joined the wind. Though something the same and shared remained, like a buzzing of truth.

Paddling back to myself through a wall of wind. I saw you there with arms wide open. You would never let me down, not even if I tried to defeat myself.

My first response was to laugh hysterically. I never anticipated Taku Arm would be the stretch of water that would almost do me in. Jeremy was right in saying that stopping would have meant failure. At that rate, and with the state of mind I'd been in, we would maybe make it to Tagish and both hitch a ride to

Whitehorse for Jeremy's truck. I imagined explaining a failed trip to my friends and family and to the university I was fundraising for—and quickly pushed that vision out of my mind. That scenario was just not an option for me, and Jeremy knew it.

"Come on out of there!" Jeremy held up Oreos and a mug of hot chocolate.

I slowly emerged from my kayak and joined him in a much-needed sugar overdose. I inhaled the warm drink and together we downed a dozen cookies. Once satiated, we woke up our cramped legs and wandered over to the northern tip of the spit, scanning the beach for unique stones to build up Jeremy's rock collection. As we stood in the shadow of "Wolf Ear Mountain," we held hands and I leaned over and kissed his salty cheek.

There, in silence, we looked up at the face of the mountain, and I thanked it for my new understanding of strength. I couldn't help but draw the comparison between how much the mountain looked like a wolf and my Siberian husky, Mya. *This time around, she must be a wolf.* After she passed, I imagined her finding a new level of wild in her next life.

> *Your ears on the jagged mountain, perked and listening to the wind. Did you catch what it was really trying to say? That everything worth anything is worth moving through the struggle, is worth accepting the plight and moving through anyways. I heard you howl one last time, a time that is forever remembered and echoed in the hollering wind.*

Back at our landing site we played another game of Tetris with our gear and the kayaks before pushing back out onto the water. When we glided beyond the spit of land, the westerly wind greeted us again, but this time it was less intense as it dissipated across the widening valley. We paddled across to the north side of the arm, then hugged the base of Wolf Ear Mountain. After a couple of hours, the landscape changed from thick treed shores alongside the bottom of imposing mountains to rocky outcrops that stretched up to rolling hills beyond. The aspen trees were scabby and some were dried up and dead. We noticed scrapings along their bark and after passing a waddling porcupine, we quickly understood who was responsible.

The afternoon faded into evening and we started hunting for an adequate camping spot. We still hadn't reached the main body of Tagish Lake but were hopeful we were close. Off in the distance, across the Arm, warm, yellow lights beamed through the growing darkness.

Jeremy turned to me, motioning with his chin and interested eyes. "Hey, that might be the lodge at the end of Tagish Lake."

"Oh yeah?"

"We could paddle over to it?"

"I don't think so. It's still so far off and getting dark." I could barely make out his facial features in the dim light of dusk. "Besides, we don't know whether we'd be welcome."

Instead of heading to the lodge, we kept close to the northern shoreline and paddled in and out of small coves to find a camp spot. After little success, we had to accept whatever came our way. Jeremy paddled into a small cove surrounded by large slab boulders, and I followed. It was challenging to beach the kayaks on the expanse of exposed rocks. We had to nose our kayaks as far up on the rock face as possible and then carefully extract ourselves from the vessels and find some kind of footing on the slippery boulders in the dark waters below. Once successfully ashore, we did a quick walk around to determine where to set up the tent.

"Okay, so it seems we have two choices, right here on this small piece of uneven ground next to the boulders and water, or up the hill on the hummocks." My headlamp flickered back and forth between the locations as I explained our options.

"There's a carpet of ground-spider webs up on the hill. Ewww—and no thanks. I'd prefer to take my chances with the water." Motivated by his fear of spiders, Jeremy made his case then stepped from boulder to boulder back down to the kayaks to fetch the tent.

While I struggled to put up and fit the tent within the small space and made our beds as level as possible on the sloping ground, Jeremy cooked dinner. Once we'd eaten, I scanned the surrounding bush with my headlamp looking for glowing eyes and rubbed my shoulders as if I felt cold, though it was still well above 10 degrees Celsius. "Hey, Babe, I'm cold. I'm going to build a fire."

I knew that animals like bears and wolves didn't like the smell of smoke and the warm glow of fire made me feel safe. While Jeremy did the dishes at the lake's edge, I collected some dry branches and sticks and built a small blaze on a rock slab near the tent. Once I got the fire going, I stood by it intently; the glow and crackle of the orange flames reassured me after such a challenging day. Jeremy was quiet and seemed tired. As soon as he was done the dishes, he headed for bed. I stayed out a little longer to absorb the fire's warmth and soaked up its protection before joining him in the tent. When I was ready to turn in, I put the fire out with lake water. Though it hissed and smoked into the dark of the night, its nurturance followed me to bed, acting like a balm of immunity to the tilted, lumpy ground I was sandwiched upon. With the fire's lasting reassurance, coupled with my exhaustion from the difficult day, I quickly fell into a deep sleep.

Rocky shores bless us, with sleep tangled in spider webs of dreams, as we drift off into a slumber of fire.

We made it to the main inlet of Tagish Lake early the next morning. As we rounded the shoulder of Taku Arm into the main body of the lake, we were surrounded by astounding beauty. The lake ran mostly north, but also south towards radiating glaciers that embellished the horizon.

Jeremy craned his head around this way and that as if trying to absorb all the magnificence at once. "Isn't it amazing that we're the only people here in this beautiful place!" His eyes were beaming.

I nodded and managed a smile but had very little energy to truly enjoy the grandeur with him. My shoulders were throbbing from paddling against the headwind the day before and my body was tired from adjusting to the physical exertion and constant exposure to wind, sun, moisture, and the dramatically changing scenes we navigated through. As we stopped to take selfies in front of the grandiose backdrop, Jeremy's face was lit with a bubbly, full-toothed grin; my lips were tightened into a half smile.

With Jeremy's keen mood alongside my own terser emotional state that morning, I was reminded of the tentative dance he and I frequently expressed in our relationship together, which oftentimes felt more like a battle. We had met at the League of Lady Wrestlers in Dawson City the previous summer. When I first saw him, I couldn't shake the feeling that I had known him for a very long time. I immediately sensed there was something karmic between us. We discovered not long after that in the 1400s, our families had been killing each other for the throne of England during the War of the Roses. Our ancestors harkened back to The House of York on my side and The House of Lancaster on his side, otherwise known as the white and red roses.

Now as we paddled together, I sensed both our togetherness and our differences, our ongoing challenges to find a shared harmony. I wondered if it would always be this way, a continual wrestling with awkward and sometimes tense moments punctuated by moments of sweet bliss.

As we entered the main stem of Tagish Lake, a cluster of small islands greeted us. They stood in a row as if guarding the entrance north. As they allowed our passing, the shores receded and the lake widened.

Jeremy paddled ahead then looked back over his shoulder at me as he steered towards the west shore. "Beauty morning, hey, Babe? Maybe we should stay on this side for now and see where the lake takes us?"

I nodded and followed closely behind him. The early hours of the day were the most inviting time to paddle, and even though I was tired, my body settled into a rhythm. I rocked from side to side in the hull of the kayak in unison with my paddle strokes, hypnotized by the unfurling slurp of the thick water curling around each paddle blade.

The distant hum of a motor on the northern horizon lifted my trance. Before long, a small motorboat appeared ahead of us. The boat turned towards us, and as it came closer, the silhouettes of two people and a dog came into view. Within moments the boat was alongside us and the driver slowed the motor down to a crawl, then turned the engine off.

The man driving the boat cleared his throat and looked over at me while the woman next to him, gently holding their golden retriever, had a wide grin of recognition on her face. "Hi, my name is Jim, and this is Sarah. Are you Kay?"

I was shocked that these people in the middle of nowhere knew my name. I paused, then put on a welcoming smile. ". . . Yes."

Sarah scratched their dog on the head and along the base of its ears, saying, "We heard your interview on the radio the other day. As soon as we saw the kayaks, we put two and two together and presumed it must be you. And hey, there's no one else out here it could be."

I remembered how awkward I had felt doing the interview from a phone booth in Atlin while Jeremy waited in the truck. I looked out across the large expanse of water taking in the evidence that we were certainly the only ones out here. Our newfound acquaintances smiled at us and while I gazed at the gentle waves, Jeremy looked up at Jim and Sarah with a grin. He seemed gleeful to have people other than me and my silence to speak with, and he was eager to share our story. "Yeah, we had a really rough start, barely made an hour the first day on Atlin Lake with the windstorm and there was a headwind on Taku Arm that almost did us in."

Sarah nodded at him. "Yeah, we heard the weather forecast. That must have been quite something."

Jim nodded in unison with his wife. "We were worried about you two. Glad you made it through all of that."

The couple explained they were heading to their off-grid cabin. We had paddled past the quaint hut about twenty minutes prior. It was the only sign of people on the lake we had seen, other than the lodge near Taku Arm.

Jeremy rested his paddle lengthwise along the bow of Hawkweed and looked up at Jim. "Are the islands up ahead a decent rest spot? It gets a little cramped in these things."

Jim looked north to the islands in the distance and pointed at the smallest one. "Yes, actually. The small island where the lake narrows is an ideal spot for lunch."

"Awesome, thanks Jim."

"Hey, you're most welcome. Well, we should be off, but the best of luck to you both." Jim exuded a kindness that Jeremy warmed to. I normally would have as well, under more energetic circumstances.

"Yes, good luck in completing your journey. It sounds so exciting." Sarah smiled again and the dog stood up in anticipation to leave.

"Thanks, you two, we really appreciate the encouragement!" Jeremy beamed back.

"Yes, thank you!" I smiled shyly.

As Jim started the motor back up and as he and Sarah continued down the lake, I could not help but mull over the strangeness of being identified in the middle of this expansive wilderness. At times before the encounter, I had felt like my identity was drifting and morphing into all that surrounded me. I—the me I knew—was disintegrating and forces all around me were starting to participate in my journey. Atlin River had brought me back into my body and made me feel alive again. The wind on Taku Arm tested my commitment. And, Wolf Ear Mountain gave me a strength I did not know I had. When Jim identified me as Kay, this expansive reality popped, and I deflated back into the unsettled woman doing an insanely long kayaking trip.

As Jeremy and I continued on the pristine water, the wind supported our progress by nudging our backs, unlike its testing nature over the days prior. We stared fixedly at the mountains, which barely changed form as we slowly fared northward. Clouds licked their peaks like darkened waves around a rocky shoreline. Before long, I started to feel shots of hunger in the pit of my stomach. In almost perfect timing, the islands ahead grew much closer. As if beckoned by the smell of grease from a diner, we began steering towards what was described by our recent visitors as the best rest stop. Before long we beached against its sandy shoreline, which jetted out into the deeper waters like a welcoming bar. We pulled the heavy kayaks onto the sand a safe distance from the water's edge and took a moment to stretch our bodies upright. It felt heavenly to bask in the feeling of standing. After placing our most prized snacks of pepperoni, granola bars, cheese and apples into a day bag, we continued inland along a barely noticeable path.

The pathway wove between small, wild shrubs and rosebushes and then through a stand of tall, slender white spruce trees. As we followed the trail, just to our right off an embankment and closer to the water's edge, we noticed a large pile of angular rocks. Further up island, about five metres from the pile, there was a rock crag that appeared to have been excavated. Our stomachs were wailing too loudly to stop and investigate further, so we continued along the path to find a picnic spot. The path ended in a small open field at the northern tip of the island. Below, waves were lapping against semi-smooth boulders. We settled on a spot in the grassy opening and sat cross-legged facing each other, with the body of the lake in sight stretching northward.

The sharp call of a gull shot down at us from a dead tree rooted along the northwest edge of the island. I looked up at the gull then over at Jeremy. "I guess we're not the only ones who are hungry." Though there were other gulls nearby, they did not preside over the island and our picnic like this steadfast steward. The gull gazed at us as we ate our snacks, so we assembled an offering of scraps for him.

I look at you with my persistent, yellow eyes embedded in a feather coat so white it splits apart blue. As I perch on this tree of the past, I also linger in days gone. My feathers are living wisdom of my ancestors who perched on the very same tree, back when it sucked water and stored sugary sap. And down into its roots beneath the rock cairn, memories of this island lay quiet, but never surrendered, as I recite them from chapters of the world beyond us.

Wiping my mouth with the sleeve of my shirt, I rose from our picnic spot leaving Jeremy to his own reveries and wandered back to the pile of rocks we had seen earlier on the trail. I stepped down off an eroded bank lined with exposed tree roots and made my way towards the pile. At closer examination, it became clear this was a purposely placed rock cairn. Thousands of rocks had been positioned in the sizeable pyramid, about four feet wide at the base and four feet tall. The rocks were aged with lichen and smelled musty. It appeared as if they had been excavated from the nearby outcrop leaving behind a seating spot, safe from blustery weather.

I began imagining early travellers of the lake and connected waterways regularly using this island as a place to hide out and rest, just as Jeremy and I were doing that day.

How many stones will it take for me to remember you in a good way? One hundred, one thousand, as many stars in the sky—however many I can find in whatever time I am gifted in this world? I will drill through rock by hand to quarry the stones, so that I may lay more down to show how truly important you were, and still are to me. We used to rest here after fishing in the rivers to the south. I remember one very stormy day where we huddled together under the spruce trees, trying to shelter ourselves from the pelting rain. I remember you telling me that you loved this island, that you felt safe here. I see you now, as

clear as ever, in your boat filled with salmon, with a smile that fills your face and my heart. I will lay down more stones, I will quarry and collect them, and I will only stop when the lake tells me I have laid down enough to remember your life.

I walked back to the wild rosebushes along the trail, and picked a few rose-hips and brought them over to the cairn. In a moment of remembrance, I placed the hips in a small circle on its summit. As I laid the offering, I couldn't help but notice that the sores on the back-sides of my fingers were growing worse. Just as I expected, the physical stress of the trip was getting to my body. It helped explain why I was so tired that morning and now my skin was showing the results of pushing it. I felt frustrated that my body was continuing on this downward spiral. "All good things come to pass." I muttered to myself as I pulled my marred hands back under the long sleeves of my shirt as if not seeing them would make the welts go away. But maybe the welts meant something more. Maybe it was a part of me asking for something? Maybe there were parts of me I had tried to hide from myself that really just wanted to speak with me?

Would you believe me if I told you, I was there all along? You may not have noticed, but I left a sign or two to show that I say hi. I feel bad for saying more, and not enough. I feel bad for burying my hope under the rocks of this mountain. Forgive me, I am but a dull memory.

Fickle and breaking is our connection. We divided and now we lay in bits, but at least all together. No bits fall outside of this place, we can only crumble within ourselves. It's okay that I am forgotten. You know, I am forgotten and remembered all the same. We can spin around this island all we want and never see the end of it. We circle around ourselves over and over again only to be reminded of the sides we've forgotten. No really, it's okay to forget, it happens. Forgetting is as much a part of this nature as remembering and deserves an equal space at the table. Just remember to remember there are many seats, and we can sit at any.

I rejoined Jeremy at the picnic spot with an efforted smile. I felt let down by my body again after noticing the sores on my hands and didn't want to bring attention to my seeming weakness. "It's a rock cairn. Looks like it was built a long time ago."

"Wow, super cool, Babe." Jeremy reached out for my hand as I sat back down next to him. I pulled away to avoid the pain of his touch. I couldn't keep it in. I would have to explain my prickly reaction.

"They're getting worse, I'm afraid."

Jeremy looked down quietly at the grass while the gull continued to watch over us with its piercing eyes.

After our pause for the rest break and some snacks on the island, and with Jeremy simply allowing things to be, allowing me to be, I started to feel a new wave of energy.

"Thank goodness," I looked over at him, "I'm finally waking up!"

He offered an affirming smile as we returned to the sandy beach.

With a renewed strength, we pushed the boats backward into the sheltered, shallow water. As we passed by the island heading north, I watched it fixedly, savouring a new view of its bluffs and trees. I nodded goodbye to the attentive gull, who maintained his perch and turned his head seamlessly, tracing our departure.

Jeremy turned to me. "Do you feel up to crossing the lake for a new scene?"

"Sounds like a plan . . . I've got enough energy now," I said, feeling lighter and eager for the next part of the day's paddle. We steered towards the eastern shore.

The afternoon was serene and we paddled quietly, absorbing the incredible surroundings. I saw the intricately defined features of the mountains. I peered through the clear water to the lake's bottom and marvelled at how its density soaked up the columns of sunlight and scattered them at playful angles. I felt the warmth of the sun on my face and the gentleness of the wind as it jostled the strands of my hair alongside my baseball cap. I smelled a subtle freshness drift off the lake's surface. The cool smell muted the taste of salt from my sweat as I licked my dry lips. I could hear humming from the top of the stately mountains that encircled the lake.

My mind and heart embraced the buzzing air and deciphered a new kind of music from this most unexpected instrument. I quietly hummed the cryptic tunes that played off the mountains, then mustered the courage to open my mouth and add sounds. Jeremy was paddling some distance from me now, so I felt I could be bolder with my captivation. Louder and louder, I sang the surreal chants, imagining I was connecting back to my long-lost cultural origins. Were my ancestors out there somewhere?

I had never known my extended family and was ashamed of my British heritage ever since I became more aware of Britain's longstanding colonial history, which had both destroyed and changed so many peoples' lives across the globe. In fact, for most of my life, I had made efforts to run away from my culture and didn't want anything to do with it. Interestingly, when I started working for the First Nation, I was inspired by their pride and affinity for their own culture and found myself wondering more about my own. Even though I was fearful of what I might find, I decided to research my origins. As I dug back in time, I discovered that my family had originated from a land-based pagan culture. Knowing this offered me some solace because pagans were people of the land with strong spiritual connections so I could feel prouder about those associations. After reaching out to my long-lost uncle in England to ask him about ancestral cultural symbols I might include in my artwork, he encouraged me to get some runes to represent my mother's family's origin. The runes, or set of stones that echoed back to pagan times, were etched with different symbols that had both linguistic and mystical meanings. The pagans considered them God's alphabet and people believed the symbols on the runes were powerful messages of divine wisdom. The God Odin chose to sacrifice himself in order to understand the runes to gain his wisdom. He hung himself upside down on Yggdrasil, the tree of life, without food or water for nine days and nine nights and stared downward into the Well or Urd, the runes native origins. His choice to undertake transformative suffering gifted him with visions of the runes and their related wisdom. Like Odin, I had always been an inquirer of knowledge and understanding and was attracted to the spiritual mysteries of life. His story of accepting suffering for insight reminded me of my own character trait of choosing the harder, or less worn path in life. By living this way, I had acquired wisdoms I wouldn't have otherwise encountered. Odin's sacrifice for wisdom also reminded me of my desire to undertake this kayaking journey in the first place. I had started with a nagging feeling that something was out there for me, something healing and wise, and that my encounters with whatever it was, would be important for my growing awareness. I had already experienced reflections and encounters with the natural world, Mya, aspects of myself, Jeremy and other presences along this journey that felt transformative, like I was opening up to a new way of being. These experiences hadn't been without sacrifice. The toll on my body from the repetitive paddling and exposure to the elements was real. And the risks involved with entering remote wilderness with limited experience were real and deeply challenging for me.

As I dug into the mythology of Odin further, I also discovered the God had two wolves and two ravens that accompanied him. These same animals also played important roles in the Tr'ondëk Hwëch'in First Nation culture back in Dawson. The Tr'ondëk Hwëch'in had both a wolf and raven clan to distinguish family and spiritual ties, and they would display symbols of these animals in their beading and artwork. This similarity between our cultures surprised me, because at first take, I believed they were entirely different.

I continued to sing out loud, trancelike and rhythmic, and matched my paddle strokes to the unknown, yet strangely familiar anthem. This time Jeremy caught the sound of my voice on the wind and turned back to me with a great, big smile.

Hours passed and we again crossed the lake for a different view. Back on the west side, we paddled by a rare sighting of a homestead surrounded by a large green space of mostly field. The lake narrowed and the water was calm.

Jeremy started surveying the landscape as if trying to remember something. "Hmm. We must be getting close to the arm."

I took my glasses off, rubbed my eyes, then put the delicate frames back on. "We've been paddling an awful long way. It would make sense that we're close by now."

We continued past a few islands that dotted the narrow passage. As the peaceful day slipped beyond us, we turned to each other occasionally and smiled as if agreeing to the serenity of our surroundings. It was soothing to experience these sweet, spontaneous moments of harmony together; it was as if the quiet magnificence of our surroundings allowed us to paddle alongside in such resonance. Dusk arrived and the wind picked up slightly.

Jeremy continued to scan the shorelines and then turned to me. "Well, still no arm, but seems like a good time to start looking for a camp spot. My shoulder is killing me."

"Sure, sounds good. I hope your shoulder's okay." I started to peer more closely at the shorelines too. "Look!" I pointed across the lake at an open aspen slope. A mother black bear and her two cubs were running away from us diagonally up the hill. The mother first, then the two cubs loping behind her. "Well, guess we're not camping anywhere near there," responded Jeremy. My excitement about the wildlife encounter dimmed a little hearing Jeremy's comment. It was getting dark and we would be pulling over to camp soon. He was right, this was the last kind of company we wanted nearby, but although we were a great distance away, the bears seemed to know we were there and were wasting no time in making more space between us. It was the very avoidance behaviour we wanted to see.

The wind stiffened and the lake opened up before us, with arms running northwest and east ahead of us. Jeremy looked left then right, removed his cap, and scratched his brow. "Uh, this could be Windy Arm."

I looked over at him. His features were becoming fuzzier with each minute of fading light. "Well, what other arm could it be?"

"I dunno, sassy. I'm not totally sure yet." Although Jeremy's voice was sarcastic, I could just make out his eyes narrowing towards me and his shoulders tightened upwards before beginning to steer to the right. "Let's cross over and check out what's down the arm. Maybe there's a good camping spot just behind that point."

"Okay, okay. I wasn't trying to be mean; I just don't get how you can't remember. I wish you'd remember more."

I feel like I need you to have the answers for me out here. I'm not prepared and want you to fill in the gaps. But, every time I try to get through to you, it comes out all wrong and you run away. It's like an echo and then another echo before we can even start to hear each other. I steered the nose of Sugar Snap towards the point and started paddling.

Mimicking the bears, we ferried diagonally across the lake towards the rocky point at the mouth of the eastern arm. The wind was stronger in the open water, so we paddled hard to make it to the other side. Once around the point, we ventured down the arm, staying close to the southern shore in search of a camp spot. The first point seemed too high and exposed for camping and there was nowhere to beach our kayaks.

Jeremy pointed a little further down from the point on the south shore. "How about just down there? We really should be stopping now; it's dark. I don't like paddling after dark."

I shifted in my seat, uncomfortable after the long day. "It's not good enough. We need to go further. I think there's a better site ahead. We can use the headlamps." Jeremy let out a sigh of frustration and paddled towards me.

We rafted our boats together for stability and dug our headlamps out from the small compartments behind our seats before strapping them on. With the comfort of having an extended light source, I paddled out ahead of Jeremy, eager to show him the perfect campsite. *If you can't give me what I need, I'll take charge and lead the way.*

"There!" I glanced back at the ball of light on what I imagined to be Jeremy's forehead. "Just ahead!"

In a stroke of luck, I found the perfect campsite. It was on a protruding rock bluff, complete with trees for protection and a pebbled beach for our kayaks. I paddled hastily towards the beach and Jeremy followed sluggishly. Once ashore, we began unpacking and hiking our supplies uphill to the flat spot on the rock bluff. It wasn't until we were putting up the tent that I realized how tired I was.

Jeremy clicked the tent poles together with a grimace. "We shouldn't have pushed it like that. You knew we should have stopped sooner and you kept going to find the perfect site. It wouldn't have made any difference where we laid our heads, but it could've cost us."

I sighed loudly in agitation, but deep down I knew he was right. I had totally lost track of how tired I was and was shocked at how much fatigue had affected my decision making. I had been overconfident in my quest to find us a "better" site. I kept my head down and worked quickly to help Jeremy set up the tent and then heated up an instant dinner. I looked over at him as we shovelled gooey macaroni into our mouths. My gaze couldn't go unnoticed as the light from my headlamp lit up the side of his face.

"What?!?" His eyes squinted into slivers in the bright light.

"Nothing." I turned back to my bowl and licked it clean.

After dinner, we hastily made for bed. Jeremy laid down first and within minutes was snoring. I laid down, but could not sleep even in my weary state. As I stared into the dark at where I imagined his face to be, my ears picked up a sound in the bush. Immediately, I thought about the bears we saw earlier. Then, I heard footsteps crackling through the undergrowth towards our tent. They paused on their approach and then bolted in the opposite direction. I grasped Jeremy's shoulder. "Did you hear that?" I was hoping to receive some kind of assurance or affection from him, but instead was greeted by the rhythmic baritones of his snoring breath as he slept soundly on the thin mat on the tent floor. Without his protection, I desperately felt around my sleeping bag for the bear spray and knife and pulled them close to my pillow. As I laid there in the dark with my eyes and ears wide open and hand on my weapons, my heart sank with the feeling that I was already doing this trip alone.

Early the next morning, exhausted from lack of sleep, I emerged slowly from my sleeping bag and squinted at the nagging sunrise through the tent window. I had been wide awake thinking all night and my mind was still reeling. *Why have I taken this trip on? It is really beyond my capabilities. I still have 800 kilometres to paddle, and mostly alone. Can I actually pull it off? Not a chance.* My jagged, overtaxed mind was not doing me any favours and was acting more like a bully than a cheerleader.

I got up and out and did a quick take around our camp to make sure there were no signs of bear from our visitors the night before. *The coast is clear, at least that's something.* I cooked up some warm oatmeal for breakfast, and as soon as the goo started to boil, Jeremy rose from the tent and joined me for a bowl. We chewed quietly as we sat on the rocky outcrop overlooking the serene waters of Tagish Lake. I mentioned the sound of visitors from the night before and how he had missed the whole thing because he was passed out.

"Things sound much bigger when you're camping in the bush you know. This one time I heard a tremendous noise while camping along the Yukon River, I thought it was a massive animal walking through the river, but instead it turned out to be a tiny fish flopping along the shoreline. What you heard last night could've been a squirrel."

"Or the bears we saw earlier." *Why does he have to down-play everything?* I gritted my teeth trying to hold back seething words of annoyance.

The lake's surface chattered sweetly up to us, its arms stretching out of view west to east, as if offering a reassuring hug under downtrodden circumstances.

Jeremy paused between mouthfuls of our warm breakfast cereal. "I can't be certain this is Windy Arm. It's been so many years since I did the Dyea to Dawson

Race and even more years since I did the journey from the Chilkoot Trail back to Dawson."

Clenching my jaw, I wiped my mouth with the back of my sleeve. "Well, is it, or not?" I felt frustrated with both Jeremy and myself. *How could we have been so ignorant to not bring maps?* I was mad at myself for rushing our preparations and for trusting that I could rely on Jeremy's memory of paddling Windy Arm nearly two decades prior. *How foolish am I?* I tried to conjure in my mind the Google Maps search we did weeks prior. I imagined Windy Arm reaching west towards Carcross and east towards Tagish. Named Windy Arm for a reason, it commonly experienced gale-force winds, which prevailed down the valley from west to east. In the Gold Rush era, this section of water capsized many a boat and drowned unlucky gold rushers.

Jeremy hadn't responded to my frustrated jab, as if hoping my mood would change on its own. After sitting in an uncomfortable silence for a few moments, he made a light grunting noise and stood up, slowly arching his lower back. Then he reached down to take my bowl and looked at me sternly as I tried to avoid eye contact. "We have to make Tagish today, Kay. We've already blown my timeline. I'm going to have to leave you in Tagish and hitch a ride to Whitehorse to fetch my truck."

I gulped at the realization that today was the last day I would have his company. We hadn't spoken of this at all since our first day on the O'Donnell River, as if to avoid calling attention to any worries either of us nursed about my upcoming solo journey. A long, sharp pain rose from my chest and came to rest in my throat. I stood up and turned away from him so he couldn't see the desperation in my face. I looked out over the expansive water actively seeking some kind of reassurance, and although the lake reached out with open arms, all I could see was how far I still had to go.

By the time we finished packing up camp and placing everything back in our kayaks, my arms and shoulders ached and throbbed like I had just finished a full day of paddling. I looked over at Jeremy as he rubbed his left shoulder. The repetitive physical motion each day on the water was taking a toll on our bodies, and yesterday's very long day was also catching up to us.

Bracing my paddle between Sugar Snap and the shore, I entered the cockpit and glanced over at Jeremy. "Well, let's get on with it." He was still standing on the beach caressing his arm.

He smirked slightly then bent down to enter his kayak. I continued in haste and pushed off the rocky shoreline as if waiting any longer would turn my kayak to stone. I steered Sugar Snap's bow to the east and began paddling down the calm waters of the arm. Jeremy launched shortly after and followed me. As I looked over my shoulder at him, I noticed he was gazing back the way we came. Baffled by his lagging pace, especially because we needed to make Tagish that day, I continued to push through the pain and into the morning's light.

After paddling for about an hour, the water became more placid. It also felt as if a gentle current was helping my kayak along. Then the shorelines drew inwards and the arm narrowed. I slowed my pace and waited for Jeremy. Mirrored on the water's surface, the bright yellow of Hawkweed eventually merged with the bright pea green of Sugar Snap.

I turned to him. "Does this look like how you remember?"

He pulled his sunglasses down the bridge of his nose and looked out over the gleaming water. "Um, I'm not sure."

"Oh?"

"Uhh, it doesn't seem right."

"Crap." I looked around at our unusual surroundings. To our left a small, aged cabin emerged humbly from the thick forest. It was barely visible through the bank of high willows. In front of the cabin, a dock wiggled slightly on the water's twitching surface.

We paddled past the cabin and the arm narrowed further. Submerged weeds danced softly under the bellies of our kayaks and the shorelines softened with blankets of duckweed. Then the slough's weeds began surrounding us in a claustrophobic hug. I lifted my paddle out of the weed-covered water and braced it across the luminescent hull of Sugar Snap. A few strands of aquatic plants clung to my paddle's blades, dripping water back to their origins.

"It's a wetland!" My shrill voice startled a dozen ducks ahead of us into flight. I turned to Jeremy. "Where are we?"

Jeremy was quiet.

"How could we have gotten lost on a lake?"

> *My life displays inside out. You hear me shout, you feel my bristles and you show me thickness. I told you and now you are telling me. You force me open to speak with you. You show me tough when I am hot-headed. You ask for my faith by leading me lost. I listen fast because your announces resound me exactly as I am.*

Now, not only my arms were burning, but also my ego. We had begun our day in the entirely wrong direction. Without a word, Jeremy paddled Hawkweed in a semi-circle around Sugar Snap, and faced back the way we came. He headed towards the cabin we had passed, and like a defeated soldier, I trailed behind him. The small, weathered cabin and adjacent rickety dock re-emerged out of the bush to our right and Jeremy steered towards them.

The wisdom may lie, but it lies within us. You didn't even need to ask and I could have told you. When you are in despair your life flips and we all tumble out of the boat, as if a rogue wave capsized us. Stay still, and stop thinking. It is all your thinking that has troubled us since the beginning. You get this. I can talk with you just like this, we don't need words, only intention. I feel you understand, but maybe lack trust. Could you hold on for just a moment so that I can be the way?

"Where are you going?"

Jeremy glanced back over his shoulder at me and said nothing.

"Jeremy?"

He glanced back at me again with a stern expression. "We need to find out where we are."

He made it to the dock first and steadied himself alongside to exit his kayak. Once he was out and had secured Hawkweed, he reached down to stabilize Sugar Snap and held out a hand to help me. We tied up my kayak and made our way down the uneven planks towards a small beaten path leading uphill to the cabin.

I hold what we need to move forward, but I won't brag about it. No, I will hide in the depths of the thick willowed valleys and not speak a word. I'm afraid to make you shiver and shout when you find out. I couldn't be more real. This could make you angry and desperate. This could make you break into pieces and shoot out all corners of your hearth. I'm here yes, but not seeking the seeker. I'll let you in yes, but only on your accord, only from your inquiry. I won't stand in your way, no, but will disguise myself in a mixture of camouflage and irrelevant tones.

Before making it off the dock, a small ermine shot up from between the wooden slats on the shore. His kiwi-sized head bolted upright on his wiry neck above tense shoulders. His eyes were small, yet bulbous and they glinted in the morning's light. As quick as he arrived, the weasel dropped back between the old wooden boards. We heard him scurry through the thick brush as we made our way up the lightly tamped trail.

I am like a snake. My body weaves in and out of the willow undergrowth like a flexing serpent. No object stands in my way. I am like water.

While dining on luscious greens, I feel your arrival. The delicate hairs in my ears, tickle and vibrate. The pierce of your anger tweaks my eardrum from far away. I hear you squeak in dismay followed by duckweed rubbing against the bows of your watery carapaces.

Closer now. A sharp shattering of dry wood as your heavy bodies hack along the dock to my home. The boards wail beneath your weight. Your lips call out in thunder. Curiosity flushes me from safety. In shocks of lightening awareness, I rise. Eyes full and only open. Everything comes in bright as I take in my world. My body tightens.

Two giants clumsily gait my way. I dig deep. My toenails clench and clasp at the worn-out planks. Not the cabin dwellers I know, rather, newcomers: sinister visitors who have appeared in fervour and with only serious inquire.

·

At the cabin, we discovered the door was locked, so we searched high and low for a key.

I stopped for a moment and rubbed my palms together. "Are you sure we should be doing this?"

Jeremy continued to look this way and that, scanning our surroundings. "There might be a map in here. We need to find out where we are." "Aha!" He tipped over a small coffee can and grabbed the key hidden underneath. Then he put the key into the door's lock, jiggled the handle and the door creaked open.

We let ourselves into the slightly musty abode. As if we were detectives in search of evidence, we immediately began rummaging through books and magazines on an old shelf looking for anything that resembled a map.

Jeremy read a book title out loud as he flipped through a number of religious texts: "Hmmm . . . Our Daily Bread."

I looked around the front room and noticed a cross hanging on the wall. The cabin was in pretty good shape considering. *I wonder how often the owners come down to spend time here?* I thought, as Jeremy sifted through a pile of local tourist magazines. One after the other showed miniature maps of lakes to the north. One map included the region just north of Tagish Lake but not the lake itself.

Jeremy gave a play-by-play as he flipped through the magazines one after the other. "Maybe this one? No. . . . This one? No. . . ." Then, "Aha!" He pulled out a brochure of Tagish and the surrounding area and turned it over to uncover a small map of Tagish Lake on the back.

He held the map away from his face as if to check his sight. "Oh my God." He turned to me, with a dismayed look on his face.

"What? I thought you'd be happy to finally find the map we need."

"Umm."

"What is it, Jeremy?" I replied, suddenly concerned.

"We're only halfway." He passed me the brochure so that I could see for myself.

"Halfway? What do you mean we're only halfway?!" I scanned the small graphic trying to understand where we were. Jeremy came up behind me, looked over my shoulder and placed his finger on a miniscule arm of the lake that ended in what appeared to be a river.

His finger was only halfway up the blue polygon depicting Tagish Lake. "You see that arm?"

I didn't want to see it. I didn't want to know it. "Uh-huh."

"That's where we are."

"So, in other words, lost."

Take me the wrong way and let me float. I won't make it back when I should, and I won't be sad about it. Leave me a while to ponder, about which way is right and which way is fraught. Remind me. There is no easy way, for no lessons learned are no lessons taught. Forgive me for my ignorance, as I don't know upside from down. I am only a human bearing the life written in the palms of my hands. So, take me the wrong way. Do not worry and do not fret. For I have learned now, that there is only a wrong way, when I conceive it, when I believe it, and when I weep it when I get upset.

As we reluctantly retraced our route, paddling now against the current with the sun beaming down on our backs, we reached the area where we had camped the night before, and slowed to a stop.

"I need to eat something." I reached for the snack compartment behind my seat.

"Okay." Jeremy joined alongside for a flotilla and we started chewing on cheese strings and crackers.

It was hard for me to swallow the dry snacks with a throat welling in disappointment. I began to sob, exhaling half-chewed crackers and cheese across the front of my spray skirt.

"Hey, Kay, take it easy." Jeremy tried to maintain eye contact with me but couldn't hold the gaze and cast his eyes down to the water's surface. This was his last day on the water and we both knew because of our mistaken side-trip, and new understanding of our actual location, it would be an extra-hard, long push if we were to reach Tagish by nightfall.

"I can't believe we made that mistake." I put the half-eaten cheese string down and rested my shaking forearms on the spray skirt. "That cost us at least three hours and a heck of a lot of energy."

"Sure, sure, but it also helped us figure out where we are. And, what are we going to do about it now? We don't have any other choice but to keep going." Jeremy looked up from the water.

"It's just that I don't think I'm going to make this trip. I already feel like crap and we've only paddled what, like 200 kilometres? What was I thinking?" The tears were pouring down my face now, and I methodically rubbed them off my cheeks with the heels of my palms functioning like windshield wipers.

"Come on, Kay. It's a set back, yes, but we don't have a choice here. We need to keep going and try to make Tagish. You can always get out and stop there?"

The thought of throwing the towel in at Tagish stank up my mind like a dirty rag. *Quit the trip, and so soon?* I considered what Jeremy was suggesting. Not making Dawson would mean the trip failed, the impact of which would mean so much more. All of the effort and energy put in up to now would be wasted. People were counting on me to complete the journey; the fundraiser I'd organized for the scholarship would be a failure. How disappointed the donors would be, and those who heard my pre-trip interview on the radio, and my family who were rooting for me back home, and my closest friends in Dawson awaiting my return. In addition to letting others down, I would also be letting myself down. It would mean I couldn't dig deep and stick with something that meant a lot to me; it would mean I didn't have integrity. Giving up would crush my spirit and it would be difficult for me to recover. It would mean that I would have a hard time trusting myself, my inner knowing, and my path in the future. It would have long-term impacts in my life and how I would live my life after the trip.

After draining myself of my tears, I brushed the wet cracker crumbs off my spray skirt and tucked away the plastic wrappers from the cheese strings. I looked over at Jeremy with fuzzy, red eyes and spoke quietly. "Ready when you are."

"Champ." Jeremy reached over awkwardly and patted me on the shoulder of my life vest.

We pushed apart our kayaks and Jeremy led the way around the final bend of the "mistaken" arm then turned north-west, up what we now understood as the main body of Tagish Lake. I followed him closely in a kind of daze. I felt like I had nothing left to lose, and it was strangely freeing.

After hours of paddling through strong winds and large swells, we took a break in a sheltered bay on the east side of the lake. The site looked used, complete with fire pit and plywood table. Exhausted, we sat down on the pebbled beach and stared up the lake in the direction of Carcross and Tagish.

A cloud of smoke from a forest fire plumed off a mountain near the Carcross area. We watched as it billowed and changed shape, first rising directly up as if in a chimney and then spreading out like a mushroom cap. The scene offered a surreal contrast between the forest fire plume and the surrounding lark-blue skies. As the lake glinted and flashed under the mid-afternoon sun, we sifted through stacks of pebbles with our fingers to find suitable candidates for Jeremy's growing rock collection. The pile of assorted stones living between the rudder pedals on the bottom of his kayak was starting to get in his way. Once in a while, he would get a stone sandwiched between his sandalled feet and the bottom of the hull, causing him to call out in discomfort as it stabbed into his skin. After collecting rocks, we were both feeling tired so decided to take naps in the warm sun. We were lulled to sleep by the methodical sound of the waves crashing against the glistening shoreline. When we came to, feeling a tad more energized, we sipped on juice from small boxes to re-hydrate.

After a final, loud slurp, I turned to him. "Are you ready?"

"Ready as I'll ever be." I didn't totally believe him. He still looked groggy from the nap and was moving slowly.

When we returned to the open water, the prevailing wind maintained at our backs. It felt like a strong, reassuring hand, pushing against my mid-back, as if intentionally helping me along. My arms and shoulders relaxed slightly with this additional support. Then a thought popped into my mind. *Maybe I can continue this journey if I receive outside supports? Maybe the wind is an ally, helping me on my way? What other friends are around and available to help me complete this journey?* Although my disappointment from the morning had clouded my mind and poked at my insecurities, the wind reminded me I was not alone with my efforts.

As we continued north, the smoke from the forest fire expanded and dispersed across the sky. The main plume grew, developing bulbous forms off its primary stem. The sun was beginning to set, and through the haze of the smoke the entire sky turned orange.

Jeremy turned to me. "Hey! Let me take a photo of you in front of the blaze."

In contrast to Jeremy's light-hearted enthusiasm, I was apprehensive about the choppy water up ahead, but agreed to the photo-op. Our dynamic was like a dance of push and pull and every once in a while, we would find each other again and connect in these sweet spots. I wondered if I could find him in this moment and maybe expand the connection for just a little bit longer, like a memory captured in a photograph.

I handed him my camera and paddled a few strokes away to pose in front of the surreal backdrop. I rested my paddle across Sugar Snap's hull and savoured the moment with Jeremy recognizing we would soon be up against the last and hardest push of the day to get to Tagish. While posing, I looked around at the now boisterous waters and realized we had finally reached the "real" Windy Arm. Just to the north, the lake widened dramatically, stretching west towards Carcross and east towards Tagish.

Jeremy paddled to me and passed back my camera. "One last push, Babe. Are you ready for it?"

I tried to hold in a smile because it didn't seem appropriate to smile when I felt so utterly exhausted and knew we were approaching treacherous water. "Ready as I'll ever be."

I felt Jeremy's presence close to me and, unlike our warring history, this time it felt supportive, like we were on the same side. Like warriors on the final push of our mission, we surged west into Windy Arm. As we entered the arm, the wind changed direction suddenly from prevailing south to north-west. It eagerly wailed and battered at us, as if it had anticipated our arrival. In response, we veered east to keep the wind at our backs as much as possible, staying close to the southern shore. I followed Jeremy as his kayak rose and fell in the restless waves. As I drove my vessel forward, I could just make out the inlet of Tagish River on the horizon. Jeremy steered towards it and I followed closely. I had to constantly correct my course against the strong side wind and distressed waves. Although my shoulders responded in searing pain and my core ached, I mustered a strength I had not known before. A strength buried so deep that I could only come to know it under such extreme conditions. Again and again, I committed to forging ahead as if this were my last stand. My eyes were focused and unwavering on my target, the inlet of Tagish River. *I am going to make it.*

In this moment of assurance, the wisp of a cloud dropped down from the sky directly in front of me. I watched it intently and the forms in the cloud created clear images. First a young woman and her dog appeared, reminiscent of myself and Mya. Then the cloud morphed dramatically, and I saw the distinct face of a large grizzly bear. My body immediately tensed, an old reaction from the memory of a near attack by a grizzly years before. Then unexpectedly, my fear transformed into a calm knowing. An even older memory came drifting in. *The bear is not my destroyer; she is my protector.* Reassured by this returning knowledge, the cloud quickly changed again into a nondescript hovering cluster of water vapour before slipping away and towards the river inlet.

There you are. A glimmer, a spark. You broke through the haze—a never seen by me strike of Divine. I am shocked by your apparition, or perhaps shocked by my ability to see you. Am I ready? Am I safe to dip into this world while within another?

Snap—there you are and I am here too. How can we both be in the same place at the same time when we have parted? Does this mean magic or madness? Will they think I'm crazy? What is crazy anyways? A woman in a kayak without a reason for any, or all of it? Just a bunch of messed up nightmares and unrelenting dreams.

Flicker, and there you are and there you are again, changing form into my fear of opening up into a world behind my world. Flash and I must follow. I won't blame you if it brings me into harm's way, whatever it takes to feel your fur again, swift, soft and slick beneath my palm, flickering like down feathers between my fingers.

Maybe I can speak of you in one way or another so others don't find me a fool. I could talk of your pictures in the clouds. Yes, everyone sees shapes in clouds.

I paddled harder to close the gap between Jeremy and me so he could hear me over the wind and waves. "Did you see that?!?"

"See what?"

"That crazy cloud! It appeared out of nowhere. It looked like a girl and a dog and then a bear! Then it slipped away and drifted off towards Tagish."

"Ha-ha, no. You're the one with the active imagination, not me. I didn't see a thing."

You don't need to hide from me. I am your dream, but not your nightmare. Flesh out your blisters and give me your sores. I am not the destroyer, but rather will help your wounds. I have never felt lost in your afflictions. I can stay with them, until you are ready to let that go too. Don't worry, I won't break you, I won't demolish your ways, I will only hold you under the light so you might see them. I am fierce in the underworld with my teeth and claws, but I also rise to the heavens with wings on my back. I feel it all. I am in all worlds. I will not let you lose your faith. I will hold and shroud your arms in power. With me, you have nothing to be afraid of.

In the last of the daylight, we finally reached the inlet of Tagish River.

Jeremy entered the river first. "Woohoo! We made it!"

With the river's current I was able to easily close the gap between us and started to paddle alongside him. "I have to pee so bad; my gut is killing me."

Jeremy looked back at me and surveyed my face in concern. I was shaking from exposure and fatigue and it felt like my body was shutting down. "Well, we've been paddling for hours without stopping. Let's pull over at the next possible spot. Besides, you look like crap!"

"Gee, thanks, Babe," I flashed an exhausted smile his way.

The night was setting in, but we had just enough light to see a small boat landing up ahead.

"There!" Jeremy pointed out, and we headed for shore.

With our remaining strength we pulled our kayaks onto the land. I was almost hypothermic and trembling from exhaustion. After we both quickly changed into thicker, dry clothes, Jeremy held me until I warmed up.

As he rubbed my arms and back, he peered down at me. "We made it, Kay! Tagish is just down the river."

Although I wanted to cherish the moment with him, I could only hold his embrace for so long as I was busting to pee. I scurried off into the bush and when I came back, I noticed he was rubbing his left shoulder.

"You okay, Love?" I pulled him close for more body heat and placed my hand carefully over his shoulder.

"I'm just really thankful we made it to the river and we have the current on our side now. My shoulder is completely blown."

It was hard for me to accept that Jeremy was injured. He represented strength and safety to me. If he was hurting from this trip then it surely was, and would be, too much for my own body to handle.

By the time we launched our kayaks back into Tagish River it was nearly pitch-black. The light of our headlamps danced across the rivulets of its slow-moving current. Stars emerged from the blanket of the sky and a yellow crescent moon gave us some extra light to paddle by, but paddling was pretty much over for us. Jeremy nursed his left shoulder and relied heavily on the gentle current to get him downriver.

"Hey, Jeremy." I looked over at his dark figure gliding on the serene river next to me, as my own arms throbbed.

"Yes, Babe?" The bright globe of his headlamp stared back.

"I hope you know how much you being here means to me, especially in the dark." My voice trembled a little.

"I'm so glad I get to be here with you. . . Maybe more than you can know." The light from his headlamp darted off my face as he turned forward and cast its ray across the bow of his kayak and into the surrounding black.

Just ahead of us the yellow glow of sodium lights from the bridge crossing emerged from the dark. Then, just before the bridge behind the trees, lights from the Tagish River campground appeared and twinkled delightfully.

Jeremy looked over at me. "Well." I could just make out the curve of his smile in the obscured light. "We made it."

"We sure did." I smiled towards the lights of the campground.

"This is where I'll be signing off."

I felt conflicted by the bitter-sweet arrival. I was thrilled we'd soon be in the safety of the campground and finally be able to rest. At the same time, I was devastated by the reality that Jeremy would be leaving me.

"I'm sure going to miss you. I couldn't have done those lakes without you."

"I'm sure you'd have been just fine."

We continued quietly down the river and the lights of the campground grew closer.

"I sure hope they're open. Do they have a restaurant?" A gnawing feeling rose from my stomach and I began dreaming of a greasy burger and fries.

"There is a restaurant, but it's super late, maybe 11? I couldn't see them being open at this hour."

Jeremy's comments didn't extinguish my hope for a warm meal, and I paddled towards the campground lights like a moth being drawn to the afterlife. We pulled alongside the dock and with great difficulty mustered enough strength to emerge from our plastic cocoons before pulling them ashore. We got our kayaks a safe way up the bank and then wobbled our way up the hill to the main building. I noticed the surrounding campground was quiet. Most people were probably fast asleep in their comfortable beds. But, straight ahead in the main building, there was a brightly lit kitchen behind a set of large windows, and a restaurant with a table of people chatting over drinks, even though it appeared closed.

Jeremy turned back to me as I trailed behind him. "We might be in luck! It'll be nice to have our last supper together."

"Oh, stop it." I caught up to him and grabbed onto his arm, laughing nervously under my breath.

It appeared that the restaurant owners were up late entertaining friends. As we rounded the side making our way to the front entrance, we were greeted by two men and a woman sitting on a bench smoking.

The older man looked up from under the brim of his cap. "Look what the cat dragged in!"

The woman grinned and pulled her scattered hair off her face with her right hand. "Awe, Honey, are you okay?"

A warm trickle welled down my upper lip and spattered off my chin and onto the surrounding concrete. It was the familiar feeling of a nosebleed; a telltale sign I had overexerted myself. I hurriedly dredged through my pockets in search for toilet paper to dam the blood. Over the years, nosebleeds would visit me every time I worked too hard. I became so used to getting them that I could sense them even before the blood left my nostrils and would immediately go into "first responder" mode. As I stuffed a wad into my left nostril, Jeremy covered and explained who we were and what we were doing at this hour.

". . . I'm Jeremy, and this is Kay. We just got off the water from a major kayaking trip and need a little help . . ."

The older man focused on Jeremy as he shared our story. After Jeremy was done, the man paused, took a deep drag on his cigarette, and rubbed his forehead as he exhaled. "That is quite the journey you kids are on. You must be hungry."

I quickly removed an edge of the toilet paper from the corner of my mouth and looked at him with beggar's eyes. "Do you think the owners would fix us up something?"

The man looked at the woman who seemed genuinely concerned about whether or not I was going to make it. "I'm sure they will, Hun, especially you being in the shape you're in. Go on inside and ask."

We continued past the kind strangers and through the front door. The owners were sitting at a table with three guests; the group of five were having drinks and deep in conversation.

"I heard that fire near Carcross is growing."

"Well, good thing they've got a bunch of firefighters on it because it's getting pretty close to the village."

"It sure is, and blocking our sunshine. The sky is completely covered in smoke now."

"Yeah, well, hopefully it doesn't come our way. God forbid this little piece of heaven goes up in smoke."

The conversation came to an abrupt stop when Jeremy and I entered the brightly lit dining room, and the guests with backs towards the door spun around on their chairs. The owner, a middle-aged woman with bleach-blonde hair, looked aghast as she watched us nearing the table where they sat, me with bloody toilet paper protruding from my nose and Jeremy rubbing his shoulder. Our faces were beet red from the sun and wind exposure.

"Hi there. I'm Jeremy and this is Kay. A pleasure to meet you all." Jeremy had a charming voice and manner even when he was exhausted. I slunk back a bit adjusting a new piece of toilet paper and holding the bridge of my nose as the warm blood continued to seep while Jeremy made our introductions. I looked around at the modern restaurant, bar and kitchen and was completely awestruck at this state-of-the-art establishment in the middle of nowhere. "We are paddling from Atlin to Dawson and just had one big epic day on the water. Is there any way we can get some food to tide us over for the night?"

"Of course, you two. We can do that. You sure look like you need it." The owner's blond hair flashed in the spot lights as she continued past us directly into the kitchen to make up a couple of plates.

The woman's husband stood up from his chair with an empty cup in his hand and looked over at us with curiosity while he strolled to the bar. "The bathrooms are around the corner if you need more Kleenex or a hot shower."

"Thank you, sir!" My breath waffled through my white and red moustache. I had never felt so grateful for a stranger's generosity.

Jeremy and I sat down at a nearby table and shortly after two plates of sandwiches and fries arrived in front of us. I swallowed a large bite of the BLT and looked up at Jeremy as he shovelled fries into his mouth. "Honestly, I feel like these people just saved my life."

Jeremy's eyes were wide as he looked up from his half-finished plate. His cheeks were puffed out like a hamster storing seeds, so I could barely hear him. "Same."

"Like, I feel like they've given me a second shot at life!" I smiled and took another big bite of the heavenly bacon, lettuce and tomato between the two crusty slices of bread. I knew the very sustenance and accommodation from these complete strangers was giving me a chance to proceed with the journey. Without this timely and pertinent help, I wouldn't even have the energy to contemplate continuing.

Thank you for being a stranger to me. As a stranger, you are there for me and provide me food and shelter. What would I do without you? You make my dreams come true without needing to know a thing about me. If we weren't strangers, then maybe I wouldn't ask you for help and maybe you wouldn't receive me with open arms. Maybe knowingness would make us enemies, fighting battles about decisions, power and politics. As strangers, we are the best version of ourselves for each other. For a moment along our life paths, we share and love blindly.

Feeling full of food and nourished by the kindness of strangers, we set up our tent between two RVs not far from the restaurant. It was a straightforward set-up on the manicured lawn. I felt safe and secure knowing I was surrounded by other campers and well-looked-after by the campground owners and their friends. As Jeremy and I were sweetly contented but also completely exhausted by then, we decided we'd take the restaurant owner up on the enticing offer of the hot shower after a good night's rest. We both fell asleep quickly and slept solid until morning's light.

I woke feeling well-rested. The campground owners took us in again and fed us a delicious warm breakfast of eggs and bacon plus accompaniments. My body soaked up every ounce of the nutritious food. Jeremy and I wiped our plates clean, gave praise to the chef and left the dining room. I grabbed my towel and made for the showers. The hot water felt like heaven on my aching back and shoulders and I came out of the steamy room anew. The sores on my hands, with me well before the start of the trip, were gradually getting worse. I still did not know what was causing them, but surmised they were stress-related. After the shower, they presented as red, itchy blisters dappling the entire backs of my fingers. I carefully smoothed aloe gel over them and whispered, "Please heal." I couldn't afford to have my health concerns take over my body, or more importantly my mind, especially now when I needed to make the decision whether to call it quits or to keep going.

Back at our campsite, I looked more closely at the burning blisters under the light of the morning sun. From certain angles, they didn't look too bad at all.

"Hey, what'cha doin'? Jeremy had returned from the washrooms and looked at me with curiosity.

"Oh nothing." I dropped my hands and kneeled down to start unpacking the tent.

"No seriously, what's up?" He wasn't going to let it go.

"Well, it's just that my hand sores are getting worse."

"Let me see," he said, so I stood up again and showed him my blotchy, blistered hands. "Geez, those look bad. And that nosebleed last night."

"Yeah, yeah, I know. You know how I get them sometimes when I'm worn out. It's not a big deal, right?"

"Well, Babe. You still have a long way to go."

"I know." We both became silent for a moment and I felt a wall of tension build up around me in anticipation.

"So, which is it? Will you carry on, or scratch?" He looked at me inquisitively as if trying to guess what my answer would be. I gently withdrew my hands from his and knelt down again at the tent door.

I felt nauseous at the weighty decision I was about to make. Should I continue on the journey of 750 kilometres in the wilderness by myself, or be realistic about my physical state and sub-par abilities and call it quits? *Fuck, why is nothing clear. Why am I always struggling with uncertainty in myself? Why am I constantly tested to see how committed I really am to the things I desire in my life? Why do I dream big only to be tested of my patience and endurance, and my faith?* It was like I had some strong karmic ties pressing me to learn a very big lesson, but I couldn't quite understand the teaching. Was it about trusting and having faith in seeing my desire through no matter what, or about letting go of the effort and accepting the realities of my current situation, finding the path of least resistance, like a river? I remembered the question my life coach had asked me over the phone months back: *What do I know that I didn't know I already knew?* An answer formed in my mind. *A river also keeps flowing no matter what. A river creates its own way.*

I took a deep breath and looked back up at Jeremy. "Well, Babe. I didn't come this far to turn around." A glimmer of a smile sparked from my face.

Jeremy mirrored my smile, bent down, and gently caressed the top of my head and the mess of still damp hair. His kiss sent tingles down my back. "That was a big decision to make. You know I support you in whatever way you decide."

Although I felt tested by Jeremy from time to time, somehow his questions helped me better understand what was important to me. They gave something for me to push against. I was starting to understand this was one of the ways he loved me.

My very love calls me out and into my fear.

I wiped a tear from my cheek and Jeremy finished unzipping the tent door so I could enter and pack our bedding away.

After we had packed up camp, we laid out all our gear on the grass. Jeremy immediately went to gathering together all his unique stones from the beaches we had stopped at along the way and then placed them in a cloth bag for safe keeping. Now the sacred stones were out of the way, we focused on sorting through our gear to figure out which items I would need with me and what Jeremy could bring back to Dawson. Luckily, Jeremy had been able to arrange a ride to Whitehorse earlier that morning with a neighbouring camper, which meant he would make it on time to his other commitments. After picking up his truck in Whitehorse, he would return to Atlin, repack and then head north again to Dawson. Though our season was wrapping up in Atlin, we would still need to make an additional trip to shutdown the farm and collect my travel trailer.

Slowly the pile of gear got smaller and smaller, leaving only the necessities I needed for the remaining 750-kilometre solo trip. Similar to the challenges I'd experienced at our journey's beginning, I once again struggled with packing my kayak. I tried time and again to pack my gear and supplies in the most efficient way possible. Eventually, however, I stalled out, and sat blankly staring at my half-packed vessel.

Jeremy looked down at me and laughed. "If you keep this up, you'll never get there!"

"Little help?" I peered up at him from the pile and smiled.

He started placing items into the storage compartment in Sugar Snap's stern and I mimicked his actions in the bow. Before long, she was fully loaded and ready for her solo voyage. Jeremy and I grabbed the bow and stern bungee handles and heaved her heavy body across the dew-kissed lawn towards Tagish River. On the way to the dock, a neighbouring camper eyed us inquisitively.

"Where you folks headed?"

"Back to Dawson," I said, light-heartedly.

"This girl's got just 750 kilometres to go!" Jeremy said to the young man then looked back at me and winked.

"Oh man, that is quite the ways! Well, good luck on your journey."

"Thank you!" I managed a smile even though I was busting from carrying the weight of my fully packed boat.

After lowering Sugar Snap onto the weathered dock, Jeremy and I turned to each other to say our goodbyes. We stood in a half embrace, looking into each other's eyes. The morning's sunlight painted Jeremy's face golden and his whole body was aglow. In that moment, I felt the preciousness of him as if he were a rare gemstone.

"Hey, you know if it wasn't for you, I wouldn't have been able to make it to this point." I pulled in closer as I spoke to him.

He smiled down at me and his eyes began to well.

"Even getting the kayaks and figuring out how to pack them. And making it through those massive lakes in the wind, and that crazy river."

"Awe, Kay. You're a toughie; you would've been fine."

"Maybe, but if it wasn't my body, it would've been my mind getting the better of me . . . if I were out there on my own."

Jeremy moved his hands down to the small of my back. The heat from his palms felt warm and reassuring.

I leaned towards him and whispered into his chest. "You were there for me when I needed you the most."

He wrapped me tightly in his arms. His breath felt warm and gentle on my earlobe as he whispered, "I know you can do this."

Hot tears welled in my eyes as we lifted Sugar Snap together one last time and lowered her off the dock and onto the gently clapping water. As always, Jeremy steadied the kayak as I entered.

"Good-bye, Babe."

"Good-bye, Babe. I'll see you in Dawson." I mustered enough courage to look him in the eyes through the veil of tears.

Solo Journey Collective

*Goodbyes are like new beginnings. They are inexplicably interlinked.
You can't have a goodbye without a greeting or an ending without newness.*

I used the spoon of my paddle to push me and Sugar Snap away from the dock and made for the centre of the river, steering towards the light blue bridge whose bright yellow lights had been a beacon for us the night before. Looking back over my shoulder, I watched Jeremy pause on the dock for just a moment before he headed back to the campground to catch his ride. As I watched him turn to leave, I felt a sensation in my chest, like sticky chewing gum being stretched away from the centre of my heart. The emotion was intense and I was reminded of how Atlin River had washed away the walls I had built around my heart over the years. Without the thick protections around my heart, I felt more exposed to truly feeling my feelings.

Sugar Snap glided under the highway bridge and we continued around a bend. It would be the two of us from this point forward. I looked back one last time but could no longer see Jeremy, or the dock. It was a new experience paddling without Jeremy, and my mind spun to reimagine the trip without him. He had to leave the trip at an earlier point along the way than planned, which meant more kilometres for me to travel on the water alone. What would it be like not having the safety of my partner alongside? We had only completed about 250 kilometres of the 1000-kilometre trip and I was already exhausted. How could I possibly complete the remaining three quarters of the journey on my own in this tattered body?

Desperately, I turned and tried to refocus my energy on the solo leg of the journey before me. As I paddled into new territory, I continued to contemplate what it would be like without Jeremy by my side. *If it isn't going to be Jeremy, then who will help me finish this journey?* I knew I would have to reach out and into the world for help. From here on out, the few people I might meet on the trip could be instrumental to my success or failure. My surroundings even, the weather, the animals, could make all the difference.

I entered the serene shallows of Marsh Lake and took a deep breath. "Here we go." I looked down at the calm water. "And this time, it's just you and me—and Sugar Snap, of course." The lake responded with a myriad of star-like droplets, sprinkling from my paddle blades as they rose above the surface.

Although a large part of my remaining journey would be river travel, I still had three lakes ahead of me, including the infamous Lake Laberge, and I still didn't have maps. Much like Jeremy and I had had to navigate largely by instinct the first segment of the journey given our decision not to bring maps, I would need to rely on my foggy memory of our Google Maps search, weeks prior, to navigate the waterways up to Carmacks. I figured the route would be a straight forward shot, meaning getting lost was unlikely, but as I was completely new to my surroundings, not knowing exactly where I was added another dimension to my uncertainty.

In search of comfort, I tried again to bring myself back to the present moment by focusing on the environment around me. I paddled close to the western shore of Marsh Lake where the water was extremely shallow, only a few feet deep in spots. Aquatic plants wiggled in delight beneath the surface as Sugar Snap and I slipped along their tendrils in a passing greeting. The lake's surface reflected the orange hue of the sky that was still coloured by the forest fire smoke from the blaze near Carcross. Periodically, small flocks of ducks travelled across the lake. As they entered the scene, their bodies split apart the orange, leaving sharp, temporary trails of dark green.

I feel naked and vulnerable like the belly of a porcupine. I question my abilities and my inner strength. But it is in this very abandon I am able to understand my worth. I am able to access my essence. Without release and abandon, I will never know my true capabilities and the very fabric of my being. Without this palpable loneliness, I will never know who, or what, I am.

As I continued north, the sun became more direct and with the smoke inversion and timid wind, this was the first day of the trip I felt hot. Typically, the temperature would hold around 15 to 20 degrees Celsius this time of year in the Marsh Lake region, but with the greenhouse effect from the smoke cover, it felt much hotter. To recover from the heat, I sought small coves hidden by bowing trees as they offered pockets of shade and cooler air. It was well past lunch time when I found a distinct cove that was fully protected from the sun's beating rays. I paddled towards it and stopped a few feet from shore. As I stepped out of my kayak, the cool water felt like magic swirling around my calves and ankles. I pulled Sugar Snap into shore and tied her up to a secure tree branch. Grabbing some snacks for lunch, I walked up the slope and sat down. The ground was lumpy from boulders hidden beneath a thick blanket of cool, moist moss. I stretched out my legs and laid back for a moment on the uneven, spongy bed, savouring the support from the earth below. After my body had cooled down, I sat back up to look at the docile lake from the shady cove and started to munch on an apple. The branch of a nearby willow tree faithfully leaned over the water. Its leaves jostled slightly and flickered back the same light as the water. The same warm breeze caressed my tattered hair. Dapples of light refracted from the water's surface and dashed across my cheeks and weathered face.

Marsh Lake offered a kind of tenderness I had not yet experienced on this voyage. I thought back to the intensity of Atlin Lake, Atlin River, Taku Arm and Tagish Lake. Although I had learned to enjoy the adrenaline of these unpredictable and powerful bodies of water, deep in the core of my being I ached

for relief. This is what Marsh Lake offered me, a time to recuperate on this challenging journey. My first day on the water alone and I was given tenderness to help with the transition. I basked in this gentle moment between the fierceness of what I had endured and the unknown of the waters ahead.

Stay here. You can rest here.

Sweet aromas of decadence dance across the warm breeze through the open doorways of your life. Sweetness, only fruits of cherry, apple and raspberry. Fruits of your reward.

It's okay to be blessed. It's okay to live in beauty and with beauty and in abundance. I cherish you in so many ways. In so many versions of yourself. It's okay to belong.

You belong here with me in these shady effervescent arenas. My gold arms wrap you in leaves, shading out the heat of despair. Wistfully, I will soothe you, to your liking.

We are here for you when you need us the most. We will hold you and cradle you like a loved child. You don't need anything further.

As I finished my lunch, I began to wonder where Jeremy was. Had he caught his ride okay? Was he already driving past me on the highway back to Dawson? I felt so hidden in the alcoves of Marsh Lake, almost as if I no longer existed to the outside world. Like I was invisible.

Normally, I would be driving to Whitehorse for supplies along the highway on the lake's eastern shore. Once in a while perhaps, I would take a pit-stop at the Swan Haven Sanctuary and walk the exposed, sandy beach where the waves crashed, but I had never really connected with Marsh Lake. It had been a backdrop to my whizzing tires and hurried supply runs. Now on the opposite side of the lake, away from the highway corridor, I had a completely new and unique experience of her. She felt golden and reserved, and I felt lost within her, like hidden treasure.

In the soothing sways of your waters, I find a refuge. You give me the space and gentleness to transform into my newness, to venture off on my own. You show me I can accomplish my goals by trusting you will give me exactly what I need.

Where have you been most my life? I could have used your tenderness in many of my plights, harsh lessons and rough dealings. I see you now, feel you now, your warm embrace. Will you come by my side more often, with your tenderness, now I know you exist? Will you show me it is okay to rest and be sure of my abilities? To trust? I take you in one breath at a time and we paddle one stroke after another.

As I continued my day, I started to realize I was making good distance. I was surprised that not having Jeremy with me was actually increasing how far I could paddle. I couldn't quite understand why. Perhaps I was paddling out of fear of being alone, or because I wanted to close the gap between us. Or, had I found my true rhythm? The gentleness of Marsh Lake helped me along as well. Before the end of the day, I was already nearing the northern tip of the over thirty-kilometre-long lake. As I passed through her last few kilometres, large marshy islands appeared before me. They had clusters of black spruce and the occasional dead poplar tree that held raptor nests in their forked branches.

In the early evening's light, the lake's surface looked soft and fine like silk. Similarly, I felt my body smooth over and relax into my peaceful surroundings. The tranquility of my environment provided a safe place for my exhaustion to take over. My eyes begged to close and I slumped forward in my kayak to catch a few moments of complete surrender. I drifted across the water's tranquil surface and out into oblivion.

SMACK—KASPLOOSH! A sharp smack on the water's surface directly beside my kayak shocked my heart into overdrive. Immediately summoned from my slumber, I jolted upright. My eyes widened to witness the last slips of a beaver's tail disappear into the lake. Erratic ripples traveled out in all directions from his origin beside my kayak.

The beaver wove through the marshy water in the reverberating shadow of my boat as I received his message. "Wake up!"

There is no easy way around this, you need to wake up. You must make your destination and the only way to do this is to wake up. If you stay sleeping, you will not make it. It is that simple. You can either remain in the same waters in the same way of being, or you can wake up and become your journey. I warn you of your own demise. Not by some outside force, but by the force within. It is you who will stop you, you who will get in your way, and it is only you who can wake yourself up.

Invigorated by the encounter, chasing blood pumped through my arteries, across my shoulders, then down my arms and into my hands. With the rush, my fingers clasped the paddle tightly into my palms and my arms instantly pushed me forward with remarkable strength. It felt like time collapsed, and I was suddenly at the end of Marsh Lake. The highway bridge rose above me to mark its completion and the beginning of the Yukon River. I made the final bend of the lake and glided under the bridge. A family was fishing off the side of the bridge, with a youngster casting along the rocky shoreline below. I managed a smile as I passed them full throttle. They each waved at me like enthusiastic spectators, as if I were approaching the finish line.

I continued past the highway rest stop and towards a small man-made dam on the Yukon River. Still surging with energy, I paddled my kayak with ease to the sandy shore just upriver of the dam. I quickly exited the cockpit and pulled Sugar Snap up the slope through tall, coarse horsetails. In front of us, a small, sandy road looped around the horsetails, bushes and trees. I decided the best place for my camp was just uphill from the loop near some larger spruce trees.

After erecting the tent, I quickly warmed up my pasta supper and hastily consumed it before retreating to the sanctity of my dome. The sounds of highway traffic wailed from the other side of the Yukon River. I felt uncomfortable with my new surroundings and relied on the tent for security. I was nervous about camping so close to people given the rest stop nearby, but I had learned a few things about respecting my limits during the last few days of travel with Jeremy, and I knew this was the best place for me to stop, rather than tackle the dam this late in the day. The spot was neither the wilderness nor a well-used campground. It was a kind of purgatory. I tried to imagine my tent walls offered protection against any possible nosy visitors. *What if people see me camping here? What if they stop by? This could be a very unsafe place, especially for a woman alone.*

I checked for my bear spray and knife and made sure they were at the ready, just in case. I had already sent my inReach message for the day—"Staying here for the night"—so when Jeremy, Natasha and my sister Jane got the message, they would think I was fine. *The cell phone!* I reached into a small Ziploc bag and turned on my flip phone. We hadn't had reception this entire trip so I had no reason to use it, but now that I was alone and in range of reception around Whitehorse, it offered another way to communicate with the outside world. The phone was still fully charged from having been turned off. I placed it alongside the weapons in case I needed to make an emergency call. I knew that if I used up the battery tonight, I could always charge it with my solar charger tomorrow, if the weather cooperated.

After I'd wormed deep into my sleeping bag, I continued reading where I'd left off in *A Return to Love* in attempts to keep my mind away from fearful thoughts. The night grew in subtle shades of darker as I prayed for solace in my pea-green cocoon, and I closed my eyes.

Then the sound of a car's engine and the flicker of headlights. My body tightened. The headlights danced through the wafer-thin walls of the tent fabric as the car approached.

I could hear the driver's side window slide down and a young man's voice. "What are you doing camping here?" I dared not go outside to confront him. I didn't want them to know I was a woman on my own. I pulled the corners of my sleeping bag up and around my face.

Two men started laughing to one another in the cab. "There are tons of bears in this area. What are you doing? You're going to get attacked."

For thousands of years, we have witnessed this stand. You were there in battle. You were there until the end. But the battle did not end. It continued inside and out.

Brace yourself. We want you to know, that you are in the lights of heaven, holding on to your continuance. But down here you must be careful, for you are still in battle.

This one is more difficult, more subtle and more foundational to your evolution. Stay awake to the surroundings because they surround you for a reason. Be careful with your own creations. They can be as fierce as a worthy competitor.

Did you design all this? Complexity and chaos abound, just as your inner worlds slam together in a gravitational dance. Smash and boom, life. Smash and boom, wake to life, wake to your design, do not be a fool to your subconscious.

So, stay in tune to your encounters. They are brought to you to define you, to refine you, and to make you humble. Do not retract, but rather move towards their meaning.

Make sure you are intact. This is more critical than you think. This is essential to your survival.

I remained in a kind of paralysis and prayed the men would leave. After idling a few minutes in front of my tent, the car continued along the sandy road and back towards the highway pit stop.

I exhaled deeply knowing that I was safe, at least for now. I unzipped my sleeping back and looked around the tent floor double-checking for my weapons, inReach and cell phone. I grabbed my cell phone and quickly typed a message to Jeremy. "Arrived safely at the Marsh Lake rest stop. Kinda sketchy here, but okay!" He texted back quickly, which surprised me as I thought he might be in one of the dead zones along the highway to Dawson. "Wow, Babe, you made it super far! I just passed by the rest stop on my way to Whitehorse. I thought you'd still be way out there on the lake." Jeremy had been a mere stone's throw away from me while I was setting up my camp. *I sure have closed the gap,* I thought, as I texted goodnight. I tucked back into my sleeping bag and closed my eyes to try to fool myself to sleep. *Tonight, is going to be a tough one.* I rolled over onto my side and placed my hand over the empty space where Jeremy used to sleep.

After an unnerving night, I opened the tent fly to the early morning's light. Frost shards showered my face and shoulders as I emerged from the thin nylon enclosure. Formed from the water spray kicked up by the nearby dam, the frost had blanketed my tent and kayak overnight. The bright red of my tent and alert green of Sugar Snap had been camouflaged by the frost, making my camp much less obvious to the highway travellers. *Maybe the frost protected me from having any more visitors. What a relief no one else came by.* I was eager to pack up camp as quickly as possible so I could leave the unsettling purgatory.

I downed a quick breakfast, then dismantled my tent and hung the fly up on some tall willow so it could catch the rising sun's rays. The sparkles of ice slowly disintegrated in the fresh morning's sunlight and water droplets beaded on the saturated, red surface. I packed Sugar Snap with little concern of how best to fit my gear. Lastly, I tucked my still-damp tent into a plastic bag and fastened it to the top of the stern with bungees. Then, I walked over to the dam to open the boat lock. As I cranked the handles, the wooden doors edged open allowing the river water to surge into the lock. The water equalized to downstream levels, but for some reason, the lower doors wouldn't budge. It was as if this mid-world had a grip on me and wouldn't let me leave easily. But my drive to escape grew stronger still as I tried to work the lock for half an hour, with no success.

"Okay, okay, that's it." I stormed off the dam and returned to my kayak. "Desperate times call for desperate measures."

I bent down and grabbed Sugar Snap's bow handle and tugged her, fully loaded, across the sandy road and gravel and down the rocky bank to a quiet back eddy below the dam. The grit bit into her plastic hull like a hissing snake and I cringed at the potential damage. I placed the vessel into the quiet water as if it would soothe her scoured surface. "I'm so sorry girl." I peered through the cockpit into the topside of her hull like a concerned mother. "No leaks yet."

I turn out a lot differently than what you expect or want, because I am asking you to grow.

Still charged by the desire to leave, I entered my gritty kayak and pried off the rocky shore with my paddle. Sugar Snap quickly caught the current and nosed downriver towards Whitehorse. Once in the flow of the river, I felt immediate relief as I picked up speed in the swift current. *I am finally free of this place.*

As I paddled with the moving water's swells and oscillations, I felt revitalized as a crisp breeze washed across my face, cooling my tired eyes. With the fresh air came excitement about the next leg of my journey. *It will be so nice to get new eats in Whitehorse*, I daydreamed about loading up at the grocery store.

After what seemed like a short while on the river, I glided into a narrow canyon. I paused paddling to take in my new surroundings, then looked down to the bow of my boat to address the broach of Mya. "We must be in Miles Canyon. We used to love our walks here."

On either side of me, basalt cliffs rose in blocks of orange armour persisting against the erosive, turquoise water. As I journeyed through the narrow chasm, memories of Mya kept her close to me.

I had met her years before at a different time in my life, in southeastern BC. I knew I was in trouble the first time I laid eyes on her. As I looked down the corridor of kennels, I noticed her nested in a perfect ball on top of her dog house. "Uh-oh," I whispered under my breath. Unlike all the dogs who were running around in their cages or barking at potential new parents, Mya sat apart.

With leash in hand, I unlatched the gate to your pen. You jumped off your house to greet me, like an old friend. Our first walk was on a trail behind the pound into the semi-arid surroundings of the east Kootenay forest. You pulled hard on the leash the entire time, you were erratic and excited. I stayed with you and held on. After the walk, I reluctantly brought you back to your pen. But you had already forgiven me. You looked up at me with your steely blue eyes and let out a bizarre, sweet sound, a kind of sigh of gratitude. Over the next month, I walked you whenever I could. I made the half-hour drive from Kimberley to Cranbrook after work so I could see and spend time you.

"Yes, the black and white Siberian husky in the back," *I said to the front desk attendant at the pound where you were being housed, temporarily, when she asked which dog I'd come to visit.*

"She's not up for adoption."

"Why?"

"She's a problem dog. We're going to have to transfer her."

"Where to?" *I was committed to follow your every move.*

"We can't release that information."

I persisted. I continued to walk you almost every day and called the pound almost as much. I fended off other potential parents.

"She doesn't like men. She's a problem dog. She's not up for adoption."

One afternoon after work, my phone rang. It was the pound.

"Is this Kay?"

"Yes."

"Well, Kay, you're one stubborn woman, so we think this is going to work. Mya is yours."

The air became even cooler and a musky smell seeped from the rocks' aged formations. I marvelled at the columnar features and surrounding landscape as the strong current sucked Sugar Snap northward underneath a small suspension bridge.

Moving silhouettes emerged along the canyon sides; as people walked along the trails at the bluff edge, they peered down at me. Below the curious audience, I quietly passed through the slim channel of lively water. Within minutes the canyon walls receded into evasive shorelines.

I scanned the horizon from shore to shore and smiled down at my trusty green companion. "Ah, and now for Schwatka Lake. We're getting close to the big city, Sugar Snap."

A motor boat, packed with a group of people, appeared from the canyon behind us and zoomed past, heading north into the centre of the lake. Sugar Snap rode giddily in the boat's wake. Along the lake shore, clusters of people were gathered. Some sat back in camp chairs basking in the late summer's sun.

Schwatka Lake dwarfed in comparison to Tagish and Atlin lakes, and it felt domestic. When the hydroelectric dam was built in Whitehorse, the Yukon River system behind it was flooded, creating the lake. These higher water levels swallowed up the infamous Whitehorse rapids of the Yukon River, after which the city was named. I looked over the sides of my kayak into the water. Somewhere below, herds of swift mares continued to thunder and skirt the boulder-strewn depths, their manes tousling and whipping with white froth.

I continued paddling along the western bank of the lake looking for somewhere to pull off the water. I needed to portage around the hydroelectric dam up ahead to get to Whitehorse, beyond which I would continue northward. I could see a dock on the shore with a number of parked float planes waving their wings slightly as they danced on the waves. *Perfect. Just as I thought. I will pull out at the float planes.* Once alongside the bobbing dock, I tied up Sugar Snap and began unpacking my heaviest gear. I traipsed the items upslope and laid them alongside the Miles Canyon Road. Once the kayak was light enough, I pulled her off the water and up the slope too.

Now for the next big challenge: Finding a ride.

I had no plan about how I would portage around the large dam and get to Whitehorse for resupply. *Maybe I should've planned this more, but then I would've had to ask for help. Why do I feel like I have to do everything on my own?*

I looked down at my kayak and pile of gear, then up at the road. "I guess I'll have to hitchhike."

A snapping pulse, similar to what I'd felt at the campsite the night before, travelled through my body and exited through the bottom of my feet. *What if someone creepy picks me up? What if no one helps at all? What if I am stuck out here for hours or worse?* Still amidst all the mind chatter, I knew what I had to do. With shaky legs and a hopeful smile, I stuck out my thumb and tried to look casual for the sparse, oncoming traffic. Even though it was a quiet road, only ten minutes passed before someone stopped. An old dodge caravan, complete with a kayak mounted to its roof, pulled to the side of the road and a man exited the vehicle. He appeared to be in his early seventies, with a sun-kissed face and a long, white beard and even longer grey head of hair tied back in a pony tail.

He greeted me with a slight American accent. "Hi there. I'm Dale. Looking for a ride?"

"Wow, good timing! That'd be great. The only thing is I got this full kayak." I pointed over at my kayak and pile of gear on the grass. "I'm trying to get around the dam."

"No problem. We can put your kayak on top of my van beside mine, and your gear can go inside." Dale appeared to be a fellow adventurer and was sympathetic to my quandary. He pulled the van into a small parking lot on the other side of the road. With his help, I was able to manoeuvre my kayak up onto the vehicle's roof. With some creative engineering and the assistance of a length of rope, we mounted my kayak beside his, then packed my gear inside the vehicle. I noticed that the van was more like a home on wheels, complete with a miniature kitchen and sleeping quarters.

As Dale placed my tent bag on his mattress, he turned to me and said, "This is my summer home. I spend the rest of the year in Alaska."

"Neat, looks cozy!" I hopped into the passenger side and sat down on the overly soft, worn fabric seat.

Dale entered the driver's side and started up the engine. He acted a bit chaotic behind the wheel as we shuttled along the winding roads to Whitehorse. He kept turning to me and asking questions about who I knew in Dawson. It turned out that he also had spent time there in earlier days.

"Oh yeah?" Dale spun towards me while he shifted his hands up and down on the steering wheel. "I spent many a winter handling dogs in Dawson. Do you know Kyla?"

"Oh yeah, I know her, but not well." I kept my eyes on the road thinking it would help if at least one of us did.

"When I knew her, she was just a kid. All the talk on the dog scene was that she would be the next big musher."

I smiled back at Dale nervously, clenched the seat with my hands and turned back to scan the road. We continued down the long, curving hill past the hydro-electric dam and into Whitehorse Centre, then Dale pulled up alongside Riverside Grocery.

He followed me out of the van and slammed the door, which closed against the frame with a metallic clang. "I'll come in with you. I've got a few things to pick up myself."

We walked into the small grocery store together and parted ways down the aisles in search of our own goodies. I found the instant food section and eagerly pulled armfuls of boxed meals from the shelves and into my basket. Then I scanned the snack section, and found some much needed replenishments, which this time I would be keeping separate.

Before we began our journey, Jeremy and I had made a mixture of nuts, chocolate, Cheezie's, chips and dried fruit. Jeremy called this mix of all things delicious "gorp." Although the gorp seemed like a good idea, after day one of the trip, I was sick of it. Who knew one could have too much of too many good things?

All stocked up from the grocery store, Dale and I reconvened in the van. He placed his grocery bag behind the seat and looked over at me. "Okay, y'all stocked up?"

"Yep! All good here."

"You don't need any other supplies or gear while in town? I can drive you."

"Nah, I think I've got everything I need. Thanks though."

"So next stop, Yukon River?"

"Yep, back on the water for me!"

Dale started up the engine and drove across the road to Shipyards Park. He pulled up as close to the river as possible to make it easy for me to pull my fully loaded kayak back onto the water. Then, I crawled up onto the front of his van, careful not to step on the cracked windshield, and untied Sugar Snap. We gingerly off-loaded her onto the green grass and then unpacked my gear and groceries from Dale's summer home.

After all my belongings were laid out on the lawn, I turned to Dale, rubbing my arms uncomfortably. "Thank you so much for your help."

"Hey, no problem."

"You know, I feel really bad. I don't have anything to give you in thanks."

"No-no. That's okay, girl. You're on quite the adventure and I totally support what you're doing. Don't forget how I helped you on your journey. Feel free to share that."

I paused for a moment. "Wait!"

I went back to my pile of gear and grabbed my snack bag. While rummaging around, I felt the familiar and disparate shapes in my hand and pulled out a large Ziploc bag.

"Well, I do have one thing I could give you in thanks. Would you like a bag of gorp?"

His blue eyes lit up and his mouth opened slightly in anticipation. By the look on his face, gorp was the finest gift I could have ever given him.

Life is strange, I thought, as Dale drove away. *After all that fear of relying on a stranger to make my way around the dam, I get to meet a kind, unique old-timer.*

As I mulled over the effortlessness of receiving help, I looked down at Sugar Snap and the large pile of gear and newly acquired provisions and fell back to earth.

"Oh yeah . . . And now to repacking you."

Without Jeremy around as my packing coach, I wondered how I would be able to do it on my own. After a moment of hesitation, I knelt down beside Sugar Snap and started stuffing her bow and stern with malleable gear and, instead of struggling, I continued calmly by placing the next "best fit" item. The cooking pot curved around the bag of dry clothes like a well-fitted glove. The dried food and cook stove dropped into place alongside each other and the sleeping bag adjusted itself into the portal with millimetres to spare. Shortly after I began, Sugar Snap was completely packed with enough room to close the hatches without additional force. I smiled to myself compassionately and contemplated, *Maybe other things can be effortless too.*

Once she was fully loaded, I pulled Sugar Snap back into the Yukon River, and without much more than a glance back to shore, I pushed out into the steady current and aquamarine blue. The swiftness of the river took over and we drifted by the city at an eager rate. A young man called to me in excitement from the cement walk along the shore. "Ahhh good luck on your journey! Many blessings!" He waved his arms at me to make sure I got the message. His unhindered greeting reminded me I was not doing this journey alone. I could see the white of his smile from the middle of the river. Its warmth stayed with me through the transition of store fronts and box stores to farm land and thick willows.

The early evening's sun blazed in the western sky as I passed the milky waters of the Takhini River as it merged into the Yukon. Though the wildfire smoke had dissipated substantially since Marsh Lake, whatever particles remained in the sky still accentuated the colours of the sunset. It had been a long day with the additional road trip around the dam and grocery stop, and I was beginning to tire out. Luckily, I was on the Yukon River now, so the current kept me in motion—or should have. Strangely, as I rounded the eastern bend of the river, its current began to slow. I kept paddling but the work became more strenuous. An old, decrepit cabin emerged from the bush to my left, then the current stopped altogether.

I looked over at a small cluster of passing ducks. "Oh man, this feels familiar. Am I lost again?"

I was bewildered over how I could possibly get lost on the large river. *If only I had maps . . . what a dummy. . . . Well, I'm still close to Whitehorse, maybe there's cell service and I can call for help?* I dug into a small Ziploc bag in my lifejacket pocket and pulled out my flip-phone. *Two bars! I'm still in range! Wait, what?!? It's already nine?* The dusk of evening pressed in closer.

I scrolled through my contacts, selected "Natasha" and hit the green dial button. It rang twice before she picked up.

"Hello?"

"Hi Natasha! It's Kay!"

"Oh, hey! It's so good to hear from you. Where the heck are you now?" Natasha had been monitoring my progress every evening with the inReach check-ins. The GPS device allowed me to send her emails that showed my location so if something happened to me, she could organize an emergency response.

"Well, um, I'm not so sure. I was wondering if you can help me figure that out?" I giggled. "I left Whitehorse only a short while ago and now I'm on the Yukon River . . . I think."

"Haha, no problem. I'll look up that section of the river on Google Maps and see where you could be. Give me a sec. Wait—you don't have any maps?"

"Not for this section. I have maps for Carmacks north though."

"Oh, Kay . . . . Okay, I'll check it out. Hang on." I pulled out a granola bar to chew on while I waited. "Okay, I think I found it. It looks like you're on a small side-channel of the Yukon River. Hmm, you could maybe continue through if you wanted, but the passage looks slim . . . it's hard to say for certain."

I had flashbacks of being lost on Tagish Lake and shuddered. "I think I'll turn around and head back to the main channel, just to be safe."

"Okay, Linley. Good plan. You're looking for a camp spot now, I hope. It's getting late."

"Yeah, I know. I just need to get back on track first. That'll be my next priority."

"Okay, sounds like you could use a rest."

"Yeah, getting pretty tired out here."

"Aww. Even so, I'm so happy you're doing the trip. I wish I could be there with you."

"Me too, friend. Big time!"

"Awe."

"Thanks for your help, Tash."

"My pleasure. Good luck with finding your camp and call me back if you need anything else. I'll be waiting for your check-in."

I tried to ward off the onset of loneliness after speaking with my close friend and bidding each other a good night. But, as soon as we hung up, the physical reality of floating alone, in the middle of the dark wilderness, came screaming in. I so desperately wanted to call Jeremy but knew he was on a remote camping trip somewhere outside of Dawson so wouldn't have cell service. Before putting the phone back into the Ziploc, I checked the batteries. The bar displayed as a red sliver.

"Damn. Low batteries. I forgot to charge you. I better get this right."

I steered Sugar Snap in a one-eighty and paddled back the direction I came. Within fifteen minutes I reached the main stem of the Yukon River. I veered northward again and joined its unmistakably strong current. With a big sigh of relief, I continued around a large bend before the river widened into the mass of Lake Laberge. The shoreline began to recede on either side and the skyline broadened.

Directly in front of me there was an island with a small clearing, where the river and lake met. *Perfect spot for a camp.* I paddled hard, so the current didn't take me further out into the lake and just made the island's south-west edge. The plastic of Sugar Snap's bow ground into the gravel shoreline and I quickly exited and pulled her onto the rocks. After tying her up and debarking the heavier gear, I pulled her out of the water's reach and onto the flat, sandy bank of the small clearing.

The clearing was just large enough for my gear and tent; the remainder of the island was covered in thick alder bushes. I felt safe setting up my tent alongside the alder knowing I would easily hear an approaching animal. I decided to send my inReach messages right away so Natasha wouldn't get worried by my late arrival to camp. With my tent set, I picked through my new instant meals. "Hmm, interesting, dairy free." I jumped off the bank to the lake's edge and scooped water into my small tin pot, then returned to my kitchen set-up and placed it aside. I opened up the metal arms of my portable rocket stove and attached it to a kerosene bottle. Then, I turned the small metal knob left to release the gas. With the flick of a lighter, a steady, purple flame awoke, accompanied by a quietly amplified rushing noise. I balanced the tin pot of water on the stand overtop the flame and once it was boiling added the macaroni noodles. Then, I pulled out my trusty buck knife and cut up some sausage and added it to the mix. Once the noodles were soft, I drained some of the milky water and stirred in the powdered sauce mix with a small, wooden spoon. I ate straight out of the warm pot and made sure I finished the entire thing, even though it was too much for me. I had no way of safely dealing with leftovers. After washing my dishes at the shoreline, I hurried to bed under the dark blanket of the night sky. A spattering of stars embellished the western horizon, and I watched them flicker through the mesh of my tent window. Then, I lay down and wriggled into my sleeping bag. The light rustling of alder leaves hushed the late summer's air, similar to the "shhhhh" of a doting mother lulling her baby to sleep.

Why do you cry at night? Why do you wonder where your mother has gone? I won't try and make you feel better, I only want to ask the question. Your mother is you right? You are your mother. Why do you wonder and seek her outside of yourself? Why do you believe that you are not a mother? You are a mother beyond mention. You are the mother of it all. The mother of your experience, your reality. So why do you act like this is some kind of role you must search for? Why do you feel it is missing? I don't want to make you feel bad, I just want to remind you of what you already know. You can love and be loved, all the same. You don't need to be anyone else or anything else. You are enough. You are loved, bring the light from within and burn it out to the world. The sun won't set on this paradise. The light continues in your heart.

After a restful sleep, I woke early, before the sun rose over the mountain shading Lake Laberge. A quick breakfast and I packed up camp and loaded Sugar Snap for the next leg of my journey. My goal today was to paddle the length of the lake, 50 kilometres, and reach the outlet into the continuation of the Yukon River. Because of the distance, I needed to get an early start. Lake Laberge was renowned for its strong winds and large waves, so I paddled in a diagonal towards the lake's eastern shore. The last thing I wanted was to be smack dab in the middle of the giant lake when the wind picked up.

As I paddled, the sun crested the mountain and its white light refracted off the lake's now-playful surface. Although the lake was large and intimidating, I felt more at ease on this water as it was somewhat familiar to me. My sister Jane and I had paddled it in late June the year before in our attempts at the Yukon River Quest, a 715-kilometre paddling race from Whitehorse to Dawson City. Neither of us had any significant canoeing experience, other than my leisurely paddling on Slocan Lake with Andrea a decade before, and Jane and I really had no idea what we were in for. I remembered how long the lake felt to us as we doubled in our rental canoe. About three quarters of the way along, we reverted to techno music and uppers to stay awake. We didn't arrive at the northern tip of the lake until well into the night, paddling by the never-ending sunlight and ghostly stars of the subarctic summer. We were lucky we made it as far as Carmacks before we scratched. The exertion and exposure wore down my sister and me. I became irritable and Jane's body started to shut down; she could barely eat or drink towards the end of it. It took us the better part of a week to physically recover from the effort and about two weeks for us to joke about it. Occasionally, we would still reminisce over the phone about the harrowing undertaking. We would laugh and make fun of how unprepared we were, like how we didn't even have paddles until the morning of the race. Now I simply smiled at the memory out of sentimental longing for that earlier time with my sister on the lake.

After my early morning hustle, I started to feel close enough to the shore to veer north. The once brilliant sun's rays dispersed behind an ever-spreading blanket of clouds that now crossed the late morning's sky. The clouds thickened and turned grey and scouting rain drops smacked the brim of my baseball cap. Nervous about the incoming weather, I paddled strongly to cover as much distance as possible.

The first rain fell lightly and was refreshing on my sun-scorched face. After paddling in wildfire smoke from Tagish to Whitehorse and the uncomfortable heat on Marsh Lake, I welcomed the cool spattering on my cheeks. But soon, the lonely drops were a chorused downfall and I started to get soaked.

It was always slightly uncomfortable changing clothes, because it meant I had to take off my lifejacket when my kayak was most vulnerable to tip. I could swim but wasn't the strongest swimmer and had never experienced tipping in a kayak. If I lost balance and flipped the boat, I would be dunked into the icy cold water of Lake Laberge, water that stayed cold even during the warmest months of the year. The adrenaline and shock would take hold, weakening my ability to swim to shore. I would try and flip my kayak back over, but had no practice getting back in it once uprighted. Maybe I could pull it to shore with me, but my swimming would be too weak to get myself ashore, let alone a full boat. So maybe I wouldn't drown, but might get hypothermia if I made it to shore without my gear. All this said, it was time to put on my raincoat.

The waves jostled Sugar Snap as I carefully pulled my right arm out of the lifejacket, then swung the vest around my back to pull my left arm out. I had my inReach and camera in the lifejacket pockets, so I always feared dropping them into the water as I swung the jacket around. If I damaged my modes of communication with the outside world, I would have no way of calling for help if something happened to me.

With the lifejacket resting precariously in front of me, I grabbed the yellow handle of the spray skirt and loosened its seal around the rim of the cockpit. Then I blindly felt around inside my kayak for the familiar plasticky texture of my raincoat. I had stored it close by in anticipation of poor weather. With the raincoat in one hand, I loosened the spray skirt tension around my lower chest with the other. I dove my arms into the billowing coat, right then left, and pulled the beaked hood over my ball cap before zipping up the jacket tightly under my chin. During the whole procedure, I stared forward with all efforts to keep my weight balanced in the middle of the kayak, like a yogi dedicated to her posture. I pulled the spray skirt back up over the raincoat and tightened it around my lower chest. Then, I put my lifejacket back on, gently swinging it around my back from one arm to the other, and fitted the bottom of the spray skirt around the cockpit.

"Phewf," I exhaled deeply. "I'll live to tell the tale."

With the raincoat ordeal successfully over, I continued north. The lake began to churn slightly as the prevailing wind picked up from the south. Within moments, rolling waves rushed the stern of my kayak. I tried to dig my paddle into each rising wave and surf their forward swells. The waves broke around Sugar Snap's bow in searing rushes. Although the sound was intimidating, my kayak handled the watery charges with relative ease. She was doing better than me. I was tiring quickly from the battering wind and focusing hard on paddling with the persistent waves and my hands and forearms were soaked with the unpleasantly cold water.

"Okay, okay, I give in. Time for a break." I began scanning the shoreline for a place to pull over.

That's when I saw it, a giant, silver canoe aground on a rocky beach. Nearby, the tangerine flames of a young campfire danced in protest against the now steady downpour. Just upland, a tall, wiry man came scampering out of the bushes with an armload of sticks. He began feeding the fire. The man's shoulders were tight and pitched forward while he fervently focused on his task.

Friend? I was craving human connection so immediately decided this was where I was meant to stop. I paddled towards the massive canoe and beached my kayak slightly up lake of the large vessel. Awkwardly, I heaved my body out of Sugar Snap and stumbled across the beach's large, round stones towards my potential new companion. I could barely keep track of the comings and goings of the quickly moving man through my rain-spattered glasses as he collected more fuel for his humble, yet persistent fire.

"Hi!" He didn't react at all to my voice. *Maybe he can't hear me above the crashing waves?* "Hello?" This time he dropped his bundle of sticks on the flickering fire, turned towards me, and took a step back in surprise.

"Oh, hi!"

"May I join you?" I was somewhat afraid that he would say no.

"I wasn't expecting a visitor," he replied, at first hesitant. "Uh, sure thing, please do. I had to pull over in the storm because I'm soloing that beast." He gestured towards the silver canoe. "Look how much water I took on. My stuff is soaked!"

I stepped towards the canoe and peered over its sides to see a granola bar wrapper floating in about five inches of water.

"That's rough! Good thing you did."

"Yeah, you're telling me." He scampered off again but this time went to a pile of his gear, bent down and picked up a metal kettle. "Would you like some tea?"

"Oh man, I'd love a cup!" My entire body tingled with excitement at the idea of the warm, soothing liquid. My shoulders and upper back were aching, and I was shivering from the cold now that I had stopped.

The rail-thin man delicately placed the kettle on a small grill balanced between a couple of rocks over the fire. His dedication to feeding the fire had paid off and it was now crackling in resilience against the steady downpour. We sat down on a nearby log to try and absorb some of its heat. I stared deeply into the orange flames and they danced hypnotically, soothing my exhausted mind.

Dance with me. Rain or shine, dance with me. I will burn inside you like a beloved stone kissed by the heat of the sun. We can stay burning forever, if you dance with me.

I take your concerns to heart and then burn them with delight. I have no need for affections, only attention. Without you I am simply a spark, with you, I am the fire. So, dance with me.

You asked me to keep you warm and I did. You asked me to feed you and I did. You asked me to light your way and I did. I am here for you so dance with me.

I warmed your side, I held your hand and you moved towards me, I licked your fingers as you dipped in close. I couldn't have made us simpler; we are the call of the wild, we are the history, we are the civilization, we are all the things put simply.

There is no one who can extinguish your flame when you are with me, so dance with me. I am creator and lover, creator and creation, I am creator and beloved, so dance with me.

Sure, it can rain, but I can burn. Sure, it might rain, but my fire lives on with care and devotion, so please dance with me.

You don't need to be any other way, just speak your heart. Dig deep into that place where your voice resounds, and resonates like a guitar string. You don't need to be afraid of your power or your people or your place in the world, you just need to speak your truth and dance with me.

I haven't held you before and I know my own power, so I promise not to hurt you, but come a little closer and dance with me. It is nice and warm here in my embrace, enter gently and I will be forgiving, please dance with me. Come in, get closer, we can burn together no matter the weather, there is no need to be afraid of our dance. You can hold my hand while I hold your fire.

"Woah, it's ready!" The kettle boiled over and water splashed out its snout onto the surrounding flames in a set of pronounced hisses. The thin, agile man grabbed a small towel and rescued the fire from the sputtering kettle. He poured the steaming hot water into a set of blue tin mugs sitting on a nearby stump.

"I hope you like orange pekoe. It's all I have."

"Hey, that's my favourite kind, being British and all," I said as my wet face broke into a smile.

With the fire roaring and the tea underway, the man's shoulders lowered slightly and for the first time he looked me directly in the face. "The name is Derek by the way." He leaned towards me and offered his hand.

Derek's face was drawn and pocked with acne scars, and his eyes bulged slightly from their sockets. When he smiled, his canines marked his lower lips with small indentations. He didn't have any facial hair, but had a thick head of hair that was dark brown and untamed. He looked to be about my age, but seemed older somehow. He looked tired—really tired, like the kind of tired no one ever catches up on.

I took his hand and shook it gently, hoping he wouldn't grab the backs of my fingers and aggravate my sores, which had continued to get gradually worse. "Nice to meet you. I'm Kay."

He shook my hand lightly and released it quickly as if sensing he might hurt me. Then, he turned in a flash to fetch the brewed tea.

As he passed the steaming hot mug, he looked at me with some urgency, like he needed to tell me something. "I don't sleep much, if you can't tell."

"Oh yeah?"

"Well, you see, I'm a veteran, so yeah. I have PTSD."

"Oh . . . I'm sorry." I leaned towards him slightly, drawn to his somehow relatable pain.

"Yeah well . . . Sometimes I don't sleep for like a week at a time."

"That sounds brutal." I took a small sip of the tea and flinched slightly as it burned my tongue. "It must've been so hard for you to come back to a society that really has no idea."

"Yeah, no idea at all. I feel alone most of the time."

His comment reminded me of my own reoccurring battle with feeling alone and abandoned. "Hah, and then you decide to come out here in the middle of nowhere by yourself." I smiled at him through the tea's steam, hoping he understood that I was joking.

"Haha yeah, I'm a weirdo. I like it out here, I do, like it's better because I'm away from most people that don't understand, but then there are other things that freak me out."

"Oh yeah? Like what."

"Well, let's start with bears."

"Oh. Yeah, me too," I shuddered at the thought.

The rain slowed slightly and Derek took a big swig of the tea without seeming to be bothered by how hot it was. He looked over his shoulder into the surrounding bush, then back at me. "Last year I set up camp under a tarp on this very same trip. A bear showed up and kept crawling under my tarp and pulling at my feet! He wouldn't leave me alone. I had to chase him away in the middle of the night, yelling and screaming."

"Jesus, that's scary."

"Yeah, and another time, I was paddling along the Yukon River close to shore and without warning a mother grizzly charged from the bush as I floated past her. She ran right out into the river at my boat!"

"Dear God. You sure know how to make a girl feel safe out here."

Derek snickered as he finished his tea and went to pour himself another cup. The rain slowed down, but the wind was still strong.

Derek's stories made me feel anxious. I had been trying to ignore my fear of bears the whole trip, but it kept sneaking into my mind. After he recounted his experiences with bears in this very area, my lightly buried fear was now undeniable.

Years prior, when I was in my mid-twenties, my dad and I had almost been attacked by a grizzly. We were hiking a valley in the West Kootenays that I had been eyeing up for months. Everyone I had asked to go on the hike with me said no, except for my dad.

Finally, I was realizing my dream and the hike was underway. It was a beautiful day and the valley felt wild and lively. We had the company of our three dogs, two of which were just shy of a year old. They seemed as excited as us to be venturing up the bush trail. My dad and I couldn't wait to get to the ridge to see what was on the other side.

Before it happened, I had a strong feeling we would have an encounter with a bear. For months before the encounter, I had had recurring dreams about bears. Most of the dreams ended up with me wrestling with the bears in a full-on embrace of life and death. We were so close I could smell their musk and feel their wild sweeping fur against my face and arms as our bodies swirled and tangled in an instinctual battle for life.

In one such dream, I had experienced entering a bear's lair. As my dad and I were hiking, there was one section of trail that felt just like the place in my dream. All around were thick alder and willow bushes, and we were cresting the tree-line up out into the open. It felt forbiddingly familiar. I remember tensing up as we walked along the trail, but I didn't know how to bring it up with my dad.

I saw it first. The bear, perhaps a younger male because there were no cubs, was up the hill and to our right, with its coat glistening in the sunlight. He was only about 10 metres upslope from us. Once I made eye contact, he stood up on his hind legs to see what we were. He was impressive and extremely beautiful, but I had little time to appreciate his grandeur. My adrenaline started kicking in.

"Dad! There's a bear!" My voice was shrill and wavering. Before I could grab the dogs, the curious two young ones went to check out the rustling in the thick berry bushes and the older dog followed. The grizzly reacted immediately to the three dogs upon him and turned them back in a flash as they pulled their tails between their legs. He chased them down the slope and onto the trail. The dogs ran directly back where my dad and I stood in a mixture of awe and keen fear, and the grizzly thundered after them.

All my dad had was a whistle, and I had the bear spray. I tried desperately to unhinge the clip from the spray's nozzle, but my hands were numb from adrenaline and the clip kept jamming. Without a moment's care for our safety, the dogs sped past us. My dad's whistle was shrill with piercing desperation as he tried to get the bear's attention before it reached us.

"GET OFF THE TRAIL!" My dad's voice was determined and authoritative so my body easily followed his command. I stepped off the trail behind a tree that was not much larger than myself and my dad just stood there on the trail between the grizzly and me, as the bear charged forward. Dad blared his whistle over and over again in loud bursts, and then it went silent.

"Dad? Dad? Are you okay?" With jelly legs, I stepped back onto the trail and looked towards my father. The bear was maybe two metres in front of him and it had come to an abrupt stop. The grizzly looked at us both deeply, penetrating our respective sets of eyes as he pushed down on the ground with his massive paws. "Whoa bear, STOP, STOP!" We both yelled as convincingly as we could. At that, the bear huffed and turned his body away a little as if signaling to us that we could leave. We backed with increasing speed away from him at first and then starting running, whistling and yelling the whole way down the mountain.

It was the first time I had experienced an animal much more powerful than myself who could have easily destroyed me. Our lives were entirely in that grizzly bear's paws, and really, he didn't want anything to do with us.

Over the years that followed, before Jeremy and I embarked on the kayak journey, I had spent loads of time in the bush alone to try and desensitize myself to the possibility of bear encounters. Given where I lived, the bush work I did, and my love for the outdoors, I didn't want a fear of bears controlling my life. During those solo hikes and work experiences, I had numerous other bear encounters, and each of them, thankfully, ended positively. Still, even with these efforts on my part and with the favourable experiences, I continued to grapple with an underlying, guttural fear in my being from that one, really close, encounter. Now, fireside, my new friend's stories unearthed that fear, and I needed to quell it in order to continue my wilderness journey.

I finished my tea and looked up to survey Lake Laberge. From shore, it was hard to tell whether the waves had quietened down at all, but there seemed to be fewer white caps.

I looked over at Derek. "Do you want to give it another try?"

"Hmm, maybe. I guess I could always give it a go and head back if the beast can't handle it." He glanced at his large canoe on the shoreline.

"Where'd you get that thing anyway? I've never seen anything like it." I looked towards the giant, silver metal canoe.

"It was my dad's. He gave it to me."

"Oh?" We slowly walked towards the banked vessel.

Derek bent down and rubbed the side of its gunnel. "I'm in love with the idea of it, I mean it's so unique and old-school, ya know?"

"Yeah, it's something else. You must be strong to solo in that thing."

He smiled at my compliment. "It's actually pretty great on the rivers, but on a lake like this and in this weather, geesh. It's much better to wait these things out." He stood up and looked out at the rough lake.

I looked down at the waves crashing along the shore near our feet. "Fair enough."

"But, ya know, it'd be great to get along. My plan is to make Carmacks. My friends are picking me up there on Friday, so I have four days. I'm just a little worried I'll get stuck on this lake for three of them." Derek laughed and put his empty mug down.

"Well, it would be great to have the company. But I don't want you to push it."

"Not at all. Like I said, I can always turn back if it's still too rough." Derek snuffed out the fire with the remaining water in the kettle and spread the embers with his feet. Then he gathered his things and made for the canoe. "Better go bail out the beaute."

"Can I help?"

"Nah, I'm all good." He bent down over his swamped boat, scooped up the water with a plastic yogurt container and tossed it over the side. I took the opportunity to take a pit stop before heading back out on the water.

After I returned from the bushes, Derek stood up and looked at me proudly. "There, good as new!" He had removed almost all of the water from his boat. Then he grabbed the few things he had out on the shore next to the vessel and stuffed them under a large, green tarp; the result was a compact tower of all his gear at the bow of the boat.

He tucked back the edges of the tarp underneath a few heavier items and looked back at me. "Ready when you are."

I nodded with a smile at the familiar phrase, tightened the spray skirt at my ribs and pulled my lifejacket on before entering Sugar Snap. Once in the boat, which I'd waded out into the shallow waters next to the beach, I had to quickly secure the spray skirt around the cockpit to prevent the breaking waves from entering the hull. With difficulty, we pushed our boats off the shore and through the surf into open water. I was able to launch first as my kayak was smaller and easier to get through the breakwater. Once I had back-paddled far enough from shore to clear the crashing waves, I steered Sugar Snap north and looked back to Derek. He had just cleared the worst of the waves and was following about 20 metres behind.

The waves were still lively. *Hmm, not as calm as I'd hoped.* I proceeded, but kept shoulder-checking to see how Derek and his canoe were getting on. Right away it was obvious that Derek was struggling to keep his canoe on course and above the waves. I could make out his arms switching sides of the canoe and paddling feverishly to try and maintain a forward direction. The space between us grew until he eventually gave up and turned back to shore. We were too far apart and the wind and waves were too loud to hear one another, so all I could do was watch as he made his way towards the beach. I felt a pang of sadness as I quietly bid adieu to my potential new companion. He was the first stranger on my journey I had felt a connection with right away, almost like a friend.

Why had our time together been so short? This wasn't the first time in life this had happened to me. I recounted numerous occasions when I had met kindred souls, who simply passed through my life in a flash. I recalled the two young hikers I'd met on the trail near Atlin Lake that day I was out walking with our dogs; how the story of their wilderness trek to Telegraph Creek fed the fire in my own spirit. I recalled how Jeremy and I got excited together after that, and had decided to plan our kayak trip. And yet, it felt like the people I connected with the most, came and went. Or maybe it was just easier to romanticize the people I almost knew?

Although I was mourning the early departure of my friend, I knew he had made the right decision to turn back for his own safety. Still, I wasn't ready to call it quits because my kayak was handling the waves impressively, even though I felt uneasy. I decided to trust Sugar Snap's abilities over my own and continued paddling north alongside splendid rocky outcrops and cliffs. It was a mental game of letting go, rather than taking on responsibility for all of it. *Sometimes I need to let others carry me when I don't know how to carry myself.* I took deep breaths as the frothing waves smashed up against the nearby cliff faces, and I slowly urged forward.

Bit by bit, paddle stroke by paddle stroke, I made distance on the large body of water. *I must be nearing 350 kilometres by now, only 650 to go!*

Eventually, the day faded into dusk. The weather calmed down a little, and I looked around at the landscape. The scenery reminded me of my sister Jane and that epic midsummer's night paddle we endured during the Yukon River Quest the year before. On the horizon, I could see the same distant profile of a mountain we had fixated on during the race.

"Looks awfully a lot like a face, don't you think?" She looked back at me from the front of the rental canoe with a silly grin.

"Haha, yeah, I see it too. Things are starting to look a bit wacky."

"Yup. They told me about this. It's from the effort and fatigue. Apparently, it makes ya hallucinate."

"Fun!"

"Haha, yeah. There's an upside to this gruelling race after all."

Lost in the memory of our laughter, I stared off at the distant mountain's face as it looked up into the evening's sky. I remembered the landmark as a signal of our arrival to the northern tip of Lake Laberge.

Forever will be as long as you will it. I drift but do not swallow the inevitable. Force is a word, but not an outcome. We have to trust our follies, that they will lead us home.

Sorry for not being able to say this more clearly. I have not wandered much. I rest here in my ambles of life. Sweet rest, sweet life. Do you desire, what I do? The night sky to kiss against?

I haven't had much a wandering, but I have had a long time to ponder. I have rested here for millennia and drifted into an unrelenting space of foreverness. Do you believe the chants off the mountains? I can hear them and I sing with them from time to time. It may not make sense, but it feels right, you know. It feels right just to listen, and to sing with them. I am like them, but not entirely, a hybrid of you and them, you know, a bridge.

A bridge to the other worlds. I welcome you to drift with me, and I will take you gently into their breadths.

To summon, we must summon up the courage to live from our hearts. It is not easy and it is unconditional, that means without condition, without a guarantee of outcome. I must summon regardless and live from my heart. Do you know what this means?

It means faith to the degree that outcome is beyond us. Beyond the hills and the treeline, beyond the horizon, beyond the stars. Somewhere back there is the outcome and we can't see it, not even a little bit, we can pretend to see, maybe an image, or a shadow of an image, but we can't really trust our eyes, all we can do is trust the empty space in that it holds what life has gifted us, life.

Life within us is life without.

We are one and of the same. Two worlds yes, but together in the heart. That is where we commune, that is where we can hear each other mutter, like the wailing through thick water and dark spaces.

The light. It glows even when we do not see it. We must blindly accept the light as much as we are drawn to accept the dark emptiness. Yes, the light is glowing all the same, even when the light is beyond our reach, beyond the mountains, the treeline, beyond the lights from the nearby stars and out into the space behind where light does not travel, it is there and we must accept that just as readily, we must have faith that the light burns there all along, unconditionally. It burns, with or without audience. It burns for the sake of burning, not for itself, or anyone else, it burns and it glows with such ferocity and independence. It unwittingly slakes its way through the depths of consciousness to land as a sparkle in your eye.

All gods willing and we may light the way with our eyes even when we cannot see.

To experience this drifting, we must trust. We must trust in a strength far beyond what we believed possible in ourselves. We have been taught to not understand and mistrust our strength, god only knows what we would do if we came to remember our true strength, we would have very little need in the codependence we find ourselves in. We would shine from within and share our spark with everyone and all things and it would be unconditional for we would not need anything more, we would simply exist for the sake of existence itself, not even for ourselves, for the sake of the thriving spirit.

So break the way you think, if you dare. It will take you beyond your world as long as you can feel in your heart.

Often we forget to love one another and love ourselves. It is like we project our anger of feeling lost from ourselves back onto ourselves and others, as if we have taken the spark and splattered it across a blank wall of discontent. It drips and smears into emptiness and we sit there angry and crying like it has been taken from us. Don't worry, we cannot help ourselves, we desire to be misled so that we can perhaps notice something is wrong, so that we can perhaps work our way back to the source of all love.

We leave to come back.

Even leaving is part of this whole, we can't escape the Universality of this love. It is all things.

I gently pulled myself from the mountain's reflection. In anticipation of the lake's end, I paddled slightly east towards where the Yukon River was reborn. As I made my way across the last section of Lake Laberge, the wind died down entirely. The water around me became placid in the horn of the lake and the dips of my paddle blades reverberated in all directions on its surface. I stopped for a moment and looked back the way I had come. Part of me was still hopeful I would see Derek, but he was nowhere in sight. Instead, there was an incredibly beautiful and massive expanse of water that went on and on. I was awestruck not only by the splendour of the lake, but also at how far I had come. I had finished 50 kilometres in one day, in rough conditions. The sun, which now laid along the western horizon, painted the lake's surface in stripes of peach and orange. As my mind absorbed the beauty of my surroundings, my body began to relax with the knowledge I had just finished the last lake of my voyage. The rest of the journey would be assisted by the Yukon River's current, all the way back to Dawson.

I steered Sugar Snap's bow towards a familiar spit of land at the entrance of the Yukon River - last year's location of the Yukon River Quest check-point. It would be my camp for the night, and was a popular spot, so there was a good chance other travellers would be camping there too. *Welcome company,* I thought, as I came around the bend and into the Yukon River. I paddled hard towards the sandy shore, so as to not get pulled too far downstream, and there I beached my kayak. The shore's slope was gradual, so it was easy to pull Sugar Snap onto land.

Before unloading my things, I surveyed the campground and all the sites. On the other side of some thick willow, I could hear the chatter of people, so I wandered along the beach towards their voices. Four young, spritely canoers, who had set up camp at the group site, saw me approach and came to greet me.

"Hey there!"

"Hi!"

"You out here on your own?"

"Yep, just finished the lake and looking to set up camp. My name's Kay."

"This is Jack, Ben, Carli—and I'm Danny. Where'd you start your trip?"

"South of Atlin."

"Whoa, epic! We started in Whitehorse three days ago and we'll be stopping in

Carmacks. How many days have you been on the water?"

"Seven."

"Seven? Holy man, you're motoring. Where you headed?"

"Dawson."

"So epic!"

"I need to be there in five days. I have a job interview." I laughed a little at the sound of my own voice and the scenario I was in.

"Oh? Hmm."

"What?"

"Well, when we looked up how many days we should allow for Whitehorse to Carmacks, the guide said a week to ten days."

"Oh . . . shit."

"Yeah, sorry to say, but I think your chances of making it even further in less time is pretty slim. But you are on your own and you're making some serious distance. You seem motivated."

"Okay, well, geez." I shifted awkwardly from one foot to the other, then decided to change the subject. "Uhh, where you folks from?"

"Toronto."

"Wow, super cool you came all the way up here. A different world, hey?"

"Yeah, very different. It's so beautiful up here, nothing like back home. We don't have tracts of wilderness like this. Are you from around here?"

"I live in Dawson, well, kind of . . . spent the summer in Atlin. I needed a break."

"Nice. You're so lucky to live up here."

"I sure am." I smiled but felt my energy fading. "Well, super nice to meet you all. I want to set up my camp and have a snooze. So glad you're here. It makes me feel safer to be around people."

"Hey, yeah, super cool to meet you too, Kay. Good luck on your trip and making it back to Dawson on time."

"Thanks, guys. Have a good night."

I strolled back along the beach to my kayak with a sinking feeling. Jeremy and I clearly hadn't planned this trip in a realistic way. We definitely hadn't given me enough time. For a moment, I almost felt like I was in the Yukon River Quest race all over again. Even setting up camp felt like I was pushing my timeline.

I chose a spot for my tent close to the beach and just inside the trees. Then I prepared dinner with my rocket stove on a picnic table near the water. The weather was calm and the evening sky glowed. I finished my meal as the sun set. While I swallowed the last bite of instant rice and diced up sausage, I heard a familiar voice from the water. "Hey!"

I looked towards the river and saw the dark silhouette of a person in a large canoe approaching.

"Derek! You made it!"

With a giant stroke of his paddle Derek beached his canoe on the sandy bottom. "I had to wait until the storm died down, but I tried again!"

"I can't believe you made it here in such good time."

"Not bad, eh?!?" Derek slowly rose from his boat as if in pain and heaved the giant mass of his canoe onto shore alongside Sugar Snap. "I was motivated to find a good campsite tonight where I could get some rest and hopefully be around some people." He bent over the gunnels of his canoe and unloaded a few things onto the beach.

"Yeah, I hear you. Sometimes I feel like having people around will keep me safe from bears."

Derek snickered. "You know how I make sure a campsite is safe from bears?" He reached into the hull of his canoe, pulled out a rifle, and pointed it into the air. "I set off a few rounds of this!" He looked a bit mad holding the large gun and grinning wildly.

I laughed nervously, and he quickly hid the gun inside a sweater and tucked it alongside his tent bag. "Uh, but I don't need to tonight. There are plenty of people around, I feel safe here."

"I do, too." For some reason even though Derek seemed a bit off, I still felt safe around him, as if I knew him well.

Derek turned to setting up his tent. He seemed disoriented, probably from the lack of sleep, and in his stupor, he broke a tent pole. With frustration, he packed it all away.

"Never mind. I'll sleep in my canoe."

As I tucked into my cozy tent, I peered through the mesh window at Derek. He was thrashing about in the hull of his canoe trying to find a comfortable spot. Finally, he stopped writhing and called out from the beach. "Goodnight, bud. I hope you get some rest!"

"You too, Derek. I really hope you get some sleep tonight."

"God be willing."

I laid down and watched the mosquitos collect on the outside of my tent's mesh. They lifted their hind legs slightly, up and down, as if gently knocking to come in. I reflected on the day and my new companion Derek. He had a kind of resilience about him I found intriguing. He was the kind of strong that included admitting when things weren't meant to happen. When his canoe could no longer handle the weather, he didn't force it, he accepted the reality and went back ashore. He made the effort to try and was still okay to turn back, and he patiently waited for the storm to subside. Instead of giving up for the day, he got right back out there on the water when the conditions were right and kept paddling. I felt there was a lesson for me in this—in his way of being. I was glad to experience this kind of adaptable strength vicariously through witnessing him on his journey and the way he handled himself.

While he suffered from severe PTSD and anxiety, he also loved being in the bush, and he did so even though it was obviously triggering for him. He continued to do what he loved, even on his own, and even when he struggled with it. I felt our similarities in this way of being; perhaps why I felt immediately at home with him.

With these thoughts drifting through my mind, I began feeling sleepy and closed my eyes. The undertaking of the day slowly unravelled from my brain. I could hear the reassuring chatter and laughter from the city kids on the other side of the willows as I slipped out of consciousness and into a dream.

The sky went dark and a massive tsunami wave came towards us. We ran into an old frame house for protection from the wave. Then the wave hit and the house began doing summersaults within the wave's force. At first, I was scared and my body was tense and I felt completely out of control. Then I realized I was dreaming and I had some control over myself. I could not stop the wave or the spinning of the house; but I could decide how to respond to it. So, I started to dance with the movement of the wave and played the drums on the objects that were hurtling all around me. I felt strangely free and calm within the destructive chaos.

I woke up feeling well rested, like I had resolved something in my sleep. I roused from my tent and walked over to the picnic table to cook up some breakfast. Derek was already shuffling about his canoe, packing and unpacking his gear. As I tore off the corner of the oatmeal package, I looked over at him.

"How'd you sleep?"

Derek paused as he pulled a cook stove and coffee pot from his canoe and looked up at me. "Not at all. No tent means no tent fly. The buggers were at me all night."

I remembered how the mosquitos gathered in numbers on the outside of my tent the night before. "Oh man, I'm so sorry."

"All good. I'm used to not sleeping. I was just hopeful that's all."

I felt so bad for Derek, he was such an exhausted soul. But I also knew how strong and resilient he was to continue living his life amidst his PTSD and never-ending fatigue. I reflected, too, on my own resilience, which was becoming daily more apparent to me. Spending time with Derek helped me to consider that, to acknowledge it. Although he and I lived very different lives and had different challenges to face and symptoms to contend with, there was a certain kinship between us.

Derek arranged his cook stove and boiled up some coffee. Its bitter yet comforting smell wafted towards me and filled my begging nostrils. He looked up at me as he poured himself a steaming cup. "Want some?"

I paused a moment, imaging the buzz it would give me, then quickly shut down the urge. I had made a promise to myself I wouldn't drink coffee the entire trip to see if it would help my physical problems.

"Uhm, oh man. I so want some, but I'm going to pass. I need to break the addiction."

"Okay, all good. More for me!" Derek chuckled as he dropped a sugar cube into his cup and started stirring it with a butter knife.

My oatmeal was congealing on the heat, so I removed it from the burner and turned off my rocket stove. As the slurry entered my mouth, I kept reminding myself simplicity was the very thing my body needed right now. I heard a metallic rustling as Derek unwrapped a granola bar for his breakfast. *And, it doesn't look like I'm the only one not eating for pleasure,* I thought.

Derek took dismissive bites of the hard granola bar, each time crumbling bits of it onto his lap. He chased the dry mouthfuls with a few large slurps of hot coffee. As we ate our necessities in silence, the sun rose. The morning's light graced our campsite and spanned across the river's surface before us. Derek finished his coffee, stood up, and slung out the remaining drops from his tin cup across the glittering sand. He looked back at me and then out to the river again. "I'm looking forward to getting out early. It's a beauty morning for a paddle, and I love this section of river."

"Oh yeah?"

"Yeah, they call it the Thirty Mile. It's super fast and easy to read the current."

I started to pack up my kitchen. "Yeah, it'd be great to make the most of this beautiful weather and get off to a good start." It looked like Derek and I would be on the water together for a while longer after all. I was looking forward to his company and it sounded like he had river smarts that were beyond my capabilities. We started packing our things in unison, though it took me a little longer with the tent to put away. Derek busied himself rearranging the tower of gear in his canoe.

Once I was done, I stood up from my packed kayak and arched my lower back. It felt so good to be standing rather than sitting in the tight space of my kayak. I revelled in the feeling for a moment longer before returning to the confines of the pod.

"You ready?" I looked over at Derek who was standing at the bow of his canoe.

"Totally. I just need to get this beast back in the water."

He pushed his giant silver steed out into the quiet back eddy of the river. Then, he slowly stepped over the gunnels to assume his position on the wooden seat at the rear of the canoe. He paddled gently to steer his canoe into the gaining current. I followed, pushing Sugar Snap off the sandy bottom with my paddle and lowering my rudder once I reached deeper water.

The morning's light danced off the rippling river's surface, and a cool breeze wafted off the lively water and graced my face. I hung back slightly so I could watch and learn how Derek read the river. Attentively, I steered Sugar Snap back and forth across the river's breadth, mimicking every move of Derek's canoe as he meandered in constant pursuit of the strongest current. I started to understand how he was reading the water. It seemed that the most concentrated current followed the outer reach of each river bend. Derek's canoe was travelling at an impressive speed as if he were tapping into an invisible jet stream. I was amazed by how fast he could travel in his large, clunky boat and with minimal paddling. Even though I was continuously paddling my kayak, he was able to stay well ahead of me. It was almost as if Derek and his canoe were one with the current.

Soothed by the predictable weaving of the current's path, I felt relaxed and began to enjoy the swiftness and dynamism of the Yukon River's Thirty Mile. After a seemingly never-ending belt of large lakes, it was a treat to experience the vibrant current and its forward motion. I finally felt like I was getting somewhere. The breeze increased with my speed and swept across my face like a congratulatory feed back loop. The shorelines drifted by and around each corner the river unveiled a new view of wilderness.

About an hour had passed and Derek was still well ahead of me, but I could see him dragging his paddle. Then, he looked back over his shoulder at me. "Bathroom break?"

"Sure!"

He steered towards a small island ahead. The island split the river into two arms, one on either side. As he approached the island, he aimed for its pronounced point between the two arms and forcibly paddled until he beached his canoe directly on the spit. I tried to follow him to the island, but because the river's current was so strong, I was already half way down its length by the time Derek had beached. I felt a shot of concern as I paddled towards the island's flank. Sugar Snap lurched towards the rocky shoreline and although her bow scraped bottom, the current was too strong for the island to hold us. The active water whipped Sugar Snap's stern 180 degrees and pulled us backwards downriver. Sugar Snap's bow then kicked out into the main current and we spun another 180 degrees to face downstream. I corrected, and this time paddled frantically towards the island's most downstream shore. I was just able to beach Sugar Snap on the gravelly bottom before the island ended abruptly into deep, swirling water. I submerging my sandaled feet into the cold shallows and wearily pulled her pea-green hull onto the shore and out of the river's reach. I was breathing heavily from the exertion and felt sheepish that landing on an island was so hard for me, especially when Derek had no problem with it.

"Ahh, good lesson for ya!" Derek chirped as he walked down island to greet me.

"Haha, yeah, fun!" I smiled back at him shyly.

"It's all good, friend. Lesson learned. On these rivers, you have to aim for the island's spit—spot on."

I took off my hat and glasses and rubbed my eyes and forehead as if trying to integrate the lesson.

"And, if not, well, you'll be at the whims of the current."

"I see that! Well, I guess I like to learn the hard way!" I sputtered with laughter.

"Hah, there's really no other way to learn." Derek smiled and patted me on the back.

It was amazing to me that even what seemed to be the simplest thing, like landing on an island, required a keen knowledge of how my surroundings worked. There seemed to be rules to the river and the land that I wasn't familiar with yet. I had had no idea the river and land had agreements with one another. On their own, they seemed like pure elements—earth and water—but at their interface, some magic happened. Did the two elements come together? Did they adopt the properties of each other just a little bit? Or did they stay so true to their nature that when they met, the result was a collision of difference? Like a hurricane, a force that could only be drummed up through purity of difference.

I continued to marvel at the unique relationship between the river and the earth. Over the years, the river ate and took away the softest of the gravels and sands at the island's perimeter. What remained was the most stubborn of the land, the truest earth element. But did the earth the river eroded ever really go away? The material drawn into the river washed downstream, dispersed, and gathered in other areas of the river, creating new river banks and new islands with large pieces of driftwood. *The river both destroys and creates land in a persistent and perpetual rearranging of form.*

And, just as the river creates and destroys, so too does the island—the land the river must traverse, or skirt around. The island created and destroyed the river by splitting it in two; where the island was the strongest, the water had to go around. Meanwhile, the parts of the island that were not strong enough were swept away, yes, but they gradually created islands elsewhere and changed the curves, currents and course of the river downstream. So, even the materials of the island that drifted away both destroyed the river and created it infinitely anew. *The earth continues to generate the character of the river, how steep its gradient is, how fast it flows, where it turns, where it splits, and where it dams. The land and water continually create and destroy and recreate one another in a dynamic dance.*

After our pit stop, we continued down the winding, youthful section of river. As the day wore on, the river grew wider with the addition of the outflow from the Teslin River. I wasn't watching Derek's moves as closely anymore and was starting to rely on my own ability to read where the strongest current was. As the morning passed into afternoon, Derek steered towards shore where some red canoes were beached along the western river bank. Upslope from the canoes, I could just see the wooden forms of an old stern wheeler peeking through the tall, thick willow, like the bones of some massive, dead creature. I remembered then that Derek and I had our own unique journeys to travel and it didn't make sense for me to follow him anymore. He was on a much shorter paddle to Carmacks, with more time to check out historic sites, and I was on a time-limited mission. As Derek beached his canoe, he looked over at me as if to see whether I was coming too. I smiled and waved as I drifted by. There was some distance between us, so I couldn't tell if he smiled back, but he waved. There was something bittersweet about our unceremonious goodbye and I reflected upon this as the river's current took me further away from my companion. I felt detached from the ending of our relationship. Not in an ignorant way, rather with a more expansive sense of peace, that everything was exactly as it needed to be. "May we meet again," I whispered to myself. I loosened my grip on the paddle and breathed deeply, in and out. Our brief encounter was much like the inflow and outflow of greetings and departures I had experienced with loved ones throughout my life. Though Derek and I were very much on our own journeys, which had now taken us apart, there was one thing remaining and one thing we still shared—the river. The river still remained strong and ever flowing like the kindred connection I felt with Derek, a connection that still remained even as the current ushered me further downstream. I turned to the river ahead of me and although it felt a bit lonely without my paddling companion, I felt more equipped with the newfound knowledge he had given me about reading the river and was focused on making the distance.

I continued onward, paddling and following the river's swiftest arms. The day wore on and with the changing light, I felt the need to look for my next campsite. As I came around a bend, I saw a series of canoes stationed along the river's eastern bank. I paddled towards them, curious about the crowd and wondered whether there was a decent place to camp nearby. As I beached, I was greeted by smiling tour guides and a group of travellers who were clearly enjoying their adventures. Bundles of white fish and grayling hung from their boats. I clumsily walked past their brigade and into the forest where they had set up camp. Their group was large, maybe twelve people in total, and they had taken up most of the spots. I saw a young woman setting up kitchen and walked over to her.

"Hi, I'm Kay."

"Oh, hi there, Kay! I'm Amy." She reached out her hand to shake mine. Luckily, she chose a gentle grip and a short handshake. My hands were still afflicted with the bothersome and painful sores.

"Would you mind if I camped nearby?"

"Of course not, there are still some empty sites that way." She pointed north.

"Okay, I'll check them out." I walked in the direction she suggested and noticed two empty camp spots close to a boggy area. *They don't feel quite right.* I looked at the sky. *The day is still young.*

I wandered back the way I came. "Amy?"

"Yeah, oh hey, Kay. What did you think?"

"Yeah, not sure. Do you know what time it is?"

"One sec." She went into her tent and retrieved a watch. "It's six."

"Okay, still quite a lot of light in the sky. Do you know if there are any other campsites up ahead?"

"I'll check the map." She went to the picnic table and pulled out her map book. I looked at it eagerly over her shoulder, wishing I had my own. "You don't have maps?" She looked at me with surprise.

"Yeah, silly right? I have some for Carmacks north though."

"Oh. Well, I guess the Yukon River is a pretty straight run. All good." She flipped through the pages. "Okay so we are here at Big Salmon. And, looks like the next possible campsite is about 25 kilometres away. It could take you a few hours?"

"Okay, cool." I peered over her shoulder trying to burn the map images into my brain. "What's it called?"

"Cyre's Dredge."

"Okay, got it. I think I'll keep paddling and aim for that then."

"Sure, no worries. Seems like you'll have enough light and time."

"Yeah. Good to meet you, Amy. I really appreciate your help."

"Good to meet you too, Kay. And, of course. Safe journey!"

I nodded goodbyes to the others and made my way past the fisherman to Sugar Snap. The huddles of tourist travellers were absorbed in conversation amongst themselves and did not pay too much attention to my coming and going.

As I launched and entered the cockpit, I was feeling a bit weary. I wasn't certain about leaving their company, but was hopeful there would be people at Cyre's Dredge too. My motivation to make distance was strong and the clock was ticking for when I had to be back in Dawson for my interview. The thought of Dawson immediately made me feel homesick and I started to think of Jeremy and how much I missed him. I could almost feel him holding my hand. He had such big, warm hands. Sometimes they felt like sandpaper, but I found the roughness reassuring. They anchored me in safety as they wrapped around my palms and the backs of my fingers.

In a flash, I snapped out of my mixed reverie and into searing pain. I had somehow caught the back of my blistered fingers against the side of my kayak. The pain from the contact jolted up my arm like an alarm. "Ahhh, fuck! Okay, okay got it. Focus, focus. I need to stay present or else this boat is steering itself." Landing back in my body, I began to notice the river had shifted direction from due north to due west. With this change in direction came dramatic lighting. Even though the sun was low on the horizon, it remained brilliant and blinding as it shone directly into my eyes. My shoulders started to ache after the long day's paddle, and my stomach wailed about its emptiness.

Then, the wind picked up and it began to whisper through me. Lightly at first as it tousled my stray hair around my yellow ball cap, then in gusts, wailing across the bow of my kayak and through the centre of my emptiness. My knuckles turned white as I tightly gripped my paddle.

In unison with the wind, the water morphed into dark, thick, unrepenting undercurrents. Sugar Snap slowly continued downriver as I pried the plastic spoon ends of my paddle into the upswells. It felt like stirring wet concrete. The sun's white light of late day blasted off the water's surface and shot into my squinting eyes. Instead of offering a reassuring warmth, it only provided taciturn distraction. In erratic flashes of sharp brilliance, the light danced across the river's face, causing temporary spots of blindness in my vision.

The wind then gained a new strength as if fed by my uneasiness and started surging towards me, head-on across the pulsing water. With my upper body pressing against its gaining wall, I proceeded with all my being and weight to move through it. In distaste of my efforts, a shrieking gust ripped the ball cap off my head and dropped it onto the river's surface behind me. I looked back in horror as this hat had been the difference between my sight or blindness. Its fabric began to twist and turn under the churning surface. The yellow brim tipped upward slightly before it underwent a transitioning consumption of yellow to green to black.

And the wind continued.

Feeling flustered and naked without my cap, I tried to focus on the shoreline with slimmed eyes in hopes of finding a campsite. *Cyre's Dredge must be nearby,* I thought, and I began to expect it around every bend. Finally, after what seemed like hours, awkward angles of metal and wood, from a century past, jutted out at me from the shoreline in an uneasy beckon. *Finally! Cyre's Dredge!* I eagerly steered towards my hopes for refuge. As I came closer to shore, I saw that the campsite was surrounded by aging popular and spruce trees, some with tops missing and some dangerously laden with heavy branches.

I beached my kayak on the rocky shore and walked inland to the campsite. As I looked around the empty sites, my stomach twisted. It was dark amidst the tall, swaying trees, and there were no other campers. The company of musty dredge parts and groaning tree boughs were all that was on offer. The sky was growing darker and the wind was ceaseless. *Well, I don't really have any other options at this point. I need to stop for the night and can't be out on the water in this crazy wind anyway.* Reluctantly, I pitched my tent, but decided on a spot along the shoreline rather than in the unsettling campsite under the swaying trees. I struggled immensely to erect the tent in the windstorm. It was like trying to stop a hot air balloon from taking off. As soon as I had the poles erected and in place, I scrounged nearby boulders and placed them on the tent floor. Once the tent was heavy enough to stay grounded, I increased the radius of my search for larger boulders and placed them in each corner of the tent. Then, I threw all of my bedding and bags onto the tent floor and hastily scuttled inside its billowing walls to set up. *I still have to eat, damn it.*

I ventured back out into the wind storm to retrieve my kitchen. I set up the rocket stove on the down-wind side of a large piece of driftwood and used my body to shield the flame from the incessant wind. Although the flame struggled, the water in the pot still boiled and I was able to make up some Side-Kicks. The small portions of cheap, flavoured pasta designed to accompany a meal would be the centre of my dinner tonight. I shovelled the warm, gooey dish into my mouth, all the while shoulder-checking this way and that for bears. *There is no way in hell I'll be able to hear anything approaching in this gale.* I felt super alone. *Damn it, I should have just stayed at the last campsite with the tourists. Why did I have to push it this far? Why do I always have to push it? It's like I'm trying not to be a human or something. Why do I always choose not belonging?*

I cleaned out the last spoonful of quick-cook pasta and stumbled over the round rocks to the shoreline to wash my pot. I found some sand in the shallows and used it to scrub off the stuck bits. Then, I swirled the pot with river water and dumped the slurry back into the river just off the shore. *God, I hope the bears don't like Side-Kicks.* After tucking away the kitchen and food items back into the hull of Sugar Snap, I secured the rubber portal coverings tightly. *Sure hope these things are smell proof.* I found a large boulder and put it towards Sugar Snap's stern, near the rudder. Then I flipped her over to face down to the ground and carefully supported the stern on the boulder so that the rudder remained in the air protected from the ground. It was always good practice to turn over the kayak at night in case it rained. I also felt like it offered some extra security from interested bears who may want a try at my dried grub.

I hurried back to my tent like it was some kind of safe zone. Inside, I wormed my way as deep as possible into the sleeping bag. I laid down in the green cocoon and embodied a paralyzed state as the wind seemed to grow stronger yet. The sides of my tent flailed in and out like fraught breaths of a suffering lung and the strings on the tent fly beat nervously against the thin nylon walls. *This is brutal. I wish Jeremy was here. God, I'm scared and alone as fuck.* As I lay there in the growing darkness, the shrieking wind barraged my mind as the most unwanted wild beasts. Like bears, crashing through the surrounding alder bush, brushing their bristling fur along the sides of my tent, and testing the fly with their snuffling snouts. My eyes were closed, but I was far from asleep. All night the undesirable guests loitered in and around my tent. Some even ventured through the wafer-thin walls. As I lay there, I dared not move, and barely breathed, in hopes to neither be seen nor heard. If I remained still within, perhaps I would not be harmed.

Who are we anyways? I could almost be fooled to think we are your creation. Why did you invite us in? Is your life not scary enough? Might as well bring in a few grizzlies for company?

Well, I guess company is still company, even when it is ill-advised.

It seems like the power is all yours. The burning in your hands and everything. The burning of your soul. It lays on fire like a lost cloth, fallen from an unmanaged clothesline. Who let this thing burn? Someone should have been keeping an eye on the fire.

The burning of your hands, the welts, the ashes of your soul. Good thing souls are eternal right? What are you up to? All alone in the wilderness of your mind. What sucker would volunteer for such a plight? Why go there? You don't seem ready.

What? You say there is never a good time? Well, there might be a better time at least. A time when you feel even a little more adjusted in your skin.

Well, let us in then. Let us in. Let all the dark in, like it isn't even a thing.

Does the fear taste good, or shocking like the jolt from an electrical socket? Do you dance with it? Does it feel familiar or give you some kind of protection? Has it been there all along in the background, like the warp threads of a woven garment, like a complete skeleton?

You've built a life with this. Must feel familiar, or maybe a little exciting. Maybe it keeps you on the edge of your life so you can live in gratitude. The moment of appreciation for your life thuds just a little bit louder than the buzzing anxiety of your resting state.

Do you bring us in, because we are strong enough to protect you? What do you really need us to protect you from? The wild? Your wild?

Are you too wild for your own good? Does it make your existence an uncomfortable margin along the outskirts of humanity? Is that why you ended up all the way up here? All those years you weren't allowed to express your wildness? Is that why you came all the way up here, so you could finally feel wild, finally express that part of your nature without judgment or reprimand?

Did you run so far and make it so impossible to breathe so you could find some peace in your wildness? It seems to me you are finding some peace in there. Is it our wildness that helps you find some peace in yourself, regardless of how fearful you may imagine yourself to be? Do you need to push yourself beyond comfort to access some kind of peace in the most uncomfortable arena of your soul?

Our teeth clack and nails scrape, scrape, scrape into the recesses of your soul. Let the wild in. Let the wild in.

The dark sky finally lifted. Somehow, I had made it through the night. At dawn's arrival, I slithered out of my sleeping bag and sat up. I definitely hadn't slept. It felt like I was continuing a day that had never started and would never end. I suspected this might be what Derek's days were like. I rubbed my eyes and unzipped the tent fly to take a quick look outside for any intruders before leaving the protective dome. The wind was still chattering against the sides of my tent, but with less intensity. *No bears, the coast is clear.* I immediately started packing my bedding and clothes and chucked the full bags out the tent door into a pile. Then, I ventured out of the tent and started to pack it up as well. I winced at the pain from my disfigured hands as I rolled the nylon shelter into its most compact shape. It felt like they had gotten worse overnight. It was too difficult to put gloves on over the sores now. Every time I had to use my hands the lesions would get battered. It made me realize how much I depended on my hands and how important they were to my survival.

With all my possessions packed, I flipped Sugar Snap back over and pulled the kitchen out of her hull. There were no attempts at the kayak overnight; everything was still in its place. I made a quick breakfast of oatmeal, and eyed up every dark stump and root wad as I sat on the beach scarfing down the bland sustenance. My eyes blurred in and out of focus from the fatigue. *Ah, the ol' bear-stump game,* I mused wearily.

I recognized I'd fallen into a dark state, which had only gotten worse from the last night's total lack of sleep. My only saving grace was I knew Carmacks, a small town on the highway to Dawson, was not far off. My focus was on getting to the town's Coal Mine Campground, which, because it was frequented by tourists, had a fully operating diner. I believed I could make it there for lunch if I set off soon. *Oh my God, imagine eating a burger and onion rings for lunch today!* My mouth started watering even though my belly was full of oatmeal. With deep fried food as my motivation, I packed up Sugar Snap and set back out onto the river anticipating Carmacks around every bend.

But, instead of the reward of Carmacks, all I got was weather. I couldn't remember the first drop, but it became a ceaseless kind of rain. Without my hat, the smacks of water pelted my face and glasses. The droplets merged into rivulets on the plastic lenses of my glasses, completely impeding my vision. I didn't have the worst vision, but without my glasses, my surroundings were blurry. I took the defeated glasses off and continued paddling, this time into fuzzier surroundings.

I relied heavily on the river's current as it continued to urge me along even when I couldn't really see where I was going. *This is rough . . . an endless journey.* I pulled the draw strings of my raincoat's hood taught around my chin to try and prevent the rain from wiggling down my neck and into my underclothes. The unrelenting drops of rain felt like cold tears on my face, as they splattered and wormed down my weathered cheeks.

One benefit to the ceaseless rain was it cooled the painful, hot blisters on my hands. It seemed like water made the blisters worse in the long-run, but the rain offered some immediate relief to the acutely uncomfortable itchiness. The mixing water of rain and river seeped through the cracks of my erupting skin. I knew these moments of reprieve would mean additional days of pain, but at this point, I didn't care.

My eyes felt raw, especially now they were exposed to the rain's spittle. As I started to cry, I couldn't tell whether it was rain or tears on my face as torrents ran down my cheeks. The gears of my depleted brain churned into the darkest of cycles and I was barely holding myself together; the threat of total collapse was imminent. My arms throbbed in protest from every paddle stroke and my whole being yelled in a devastating hunger. My bones were used up and could barely supply my muscles with the structure needed to operate.

As the breeze blew in from the west, I could almost smell thick, diner grease. *Carmacks. The Coal Mine Campground Diner. It must be just around the next corner. I will order a burger with onion rings and a Coca-Cola.* I could feel the batter crumble in my mouth and the hot grease seep out of the loosely fitted onion rings. *Ahh, the slight crunch of lightly cooked sweet onion.* I chewed away on the greasy delights in the warmth of the diner and in the company of strangers.

But, Carmacks was not just around the corner. Around each bend was just another bend that did not arrive. The thinning faith that kept me paddling got thinner still. The land on either side of Sugar Snap, however, looked familiar, like it held memories. I was reminded of my sister Jane and how we had paddled this section of the river just before we scratched from the Yukon River Quest race. I remembered how we had arrived in Carmacks in a delirious stupor.

"Jane."

"Yeah."

"Did you see that?"

"Wha?" Her voice was trance-like, barely audible.

"I just saw a, a, a . . ."

"What?"

"I just saw an alien creature . . ."

"Oh?"

"Yeah."

"Whoaa."

"Yeah. It was standing on the edge of that island, checking us out."

"Crazy . . ."

"Hehe, yeah.

"Oh boy. Well . . ."

"It kinda looked like a giant ant."

"Yeah?"

"Yeah . . . Crazy."

"Yup."

"Fuck, I'm tired."

"Carmacks, soon."

"Yeah, just around the corner."

"Yeah."

"Ok then."

"Okay."

"Yeah."

"Yeah . . ."

In my barely functioning state, I paddled closer to the shoreline. The land flattened and spread out like an old townsite. *Must be Little Salmon.* Almost memories came rushing into my psyche. But they weren't from my lifetime or even from me. Maybe the past lingered along the banks of the river? It felt like the breeze was transporting a memory from the surrounding land and into my mind. A young Indigenous couple deeply in love. Conception of a child. The feeling of home; A long time ago.

I became even more emotional from the love I felt from this apparition, and my eyes welled up with a new suit of tears. They fell onto my cheeks and mixed with the rain. Equal parts fresh water and salt water stirring into miniature clouds.

The worn gears of my downwardly circuited brain fired again. This time the brain was demanding answers. *Why am I doing this insanely long trip? Who do I think I am to do this on my own? Why am I subjecting myself to all of this pain? Why? Why? Why?* I had no responses for these questions. "I don't know! I don't know! I've forgotten!"

As if in response to the desperate voice from the river, a young golden eagle flew from its perch on a tall spruce tree along the river bank and headed straight for me. She paused in the air directly in front and above me and Sugar Snap. She flapped her wings just enough to hold her position for a few moments. As she gazed directly down at me, her presence caused a wave of calm through my entire body. My brain's machinery clanked to a halt. Slowly my breath returned, and I inhaled and exhaled deeply. *Oh yeah. That's why.*

My friend. I know it has been a while. But I have not forgotten. When we entrust ourselves, we open ourselves to ways of being. I glow with certainty. I have not failed you. I have not started to understand the complexity of this place. I am in essence who I am. Frigid waters, drawn out across the land. Lay lines for my traverse. Where my food grows and perishes. Where I grow and perish.

I heard your cry and thought you a fledging. A young one in trouble. And then I saw you cry and settle in my presence. I won't pretend to be some kind of saint, or some kind of angel. I am me and I am here with you. I won't decide to escape or break my life sideways. I won't laugh or distort this. I won't distract you from your pain. But I will be here with you. I will be here as me in all of its simplicity and see you. I will grace you in moments. You may not even hear me or feel me. You may not even notice I have been listening and watching you from the shore. You may not know me or notice me. You may not care. I don't pretend to be a saviour or some kind of saint. I only want to show myself as me.

Forgiveness is a big word. It means letting go of the emotions someone else asked you to carry. I give you only once, the freedom of this word, but I don't pretend it is easy to forgive. You have been carrying a lot. A lot of tense experiences, a lot of saving and being saved. I don't pretend this is simple. It means emerging from the safety of pain. It means leaving the cocoon of traumas behind and stepping into your true self, which yes, can be scary and even paralyzing. I do not pretend to imagine the complexities of the human story, but I can share my story with you. It is about being and feeling the existence through my very body. I fly because I am asked to. I perch so I can see the river, its swirling currents that vary oh so slightly above the body of a fish. I imagine this story could sound simple and a little boring to the likes of you, but it is true and real. I say, true and defined. I say my original ultimate character of sincerity. I was born sincere, I am sincere, I will die sincerely. Sincerely to the life that made me. Sincerely to my young, to my hunting desire, to my presence in the sky.

I will embody my existence to the minutest detail of trueness. I will follow my life through to the tiniest detail. I will carve the sky and grasp the trees like they are my life lines. I will pierce the waters and tear the fish to uncover my truth, my essence. My abilities sing to the wind, like they are the wind. They bury my flesh like a conceding bear. I tell you now, I will live my life like the sincerity of a dream. There will be no uncovering it, because I will be raw and complete in my representation. I am it and it is me. I am the bright, burning desire to exist. To thrive. To be embodied. I am the manifestation of the dream. I am it. I couldn't be any other way in this world. I couldn't play small or pretend I wasn't an eagle. This is me and I am it. I was given an undeniable frame of reference. This is no drama, this is truth. This is completeness. I am embodying the completeness of my existence. My essence is the light behind the bend. I blast through the rain and embody the sun. I am life, it is me. I will never fail my mission to be true. I manifested because I could not be anything other than pure form and appearance.

Now, imagine yourself as me.

There you are buzzing in the middle between the worlds. It's okay, you are safe to be. You have no other choice; all other options are suicide. You are you, and that is brilliant. You cannot escape. You are desperate and you all the same. You are lost and you. You are vibrant and you. You are drenched and in pain and you are you. You are deceived and you are you. You are confused and you are you. You are deeply loved and you are you. Dismantle the belief that you can be anything else. You are you. Burn brightly like the sun behind the clouds. You have no choice. You burn brightly, even when it is raining. You burn brightly, scared, marred and out of existence. You burn brightly even when you fall to the dragons. You are immersed in your you-ness.

Then, as if knowing her job was done, the eagle continued her flight above and then behind me up into the weeping sky. I felt buzzed from the eagle's recognition and started to shiver profusely. Though I had lost all hope, it was clear to me that the eagle wanted me to persevere, hopelessly.

Without further protest, I seized my paddle and continued around the next bend in the river towards Carmacks. As soon as I re-committed to my journey, the rain dissipated and rays of golden sunlight greeted me. As I rounded the bend, a thin mist whispered across the river's surface and lifted into the glow, exposing the unmistakable, dark and angular forms of a boat dock: the Coal Mine Campground. My blood swelled and rushed into my muscles and paddled me to shore.

A couple of people wandered onto the dock and looked at me curiously as if I had magically appeared from the lifting mist. With a gentle thud, Sugar Snap greeted the wooden dock.

"Hi there!"

"Hi!"

"Glad to see you made it through all that rain. Welcome!"

"Thank you so much," I mustered. "You have no idea."

One person steadied Sugar Snap while the other reached out a hand to brace my quaking body as I rose up onto the dock. My heart chirped in appreciation from their assistance and an unabashed smile took over my face.

"Hi, I'm Sharon."

"And, I'm Dylan. We'll help you with your gear."

"Hi guys. Thank you so much. My name's Kay."

They helped me carry Sugar Snap into the treed campground.

Sharon looked over at me with a generous smile. She was middle-aged, with blonde hair and lively green eyes. "I'm really curious about the trip you're on. Where did you start? How far are you headed?"

"Started south of Atlin and heading to Dawson."

"By yourself?"

"Since Tagish, yeah." I squinted as a rain droplet let loose from a tree branch above and splattered across my face.

"Wow, that's so brave." Her eyes widened slightly.

I wiped the water from my eyes and snickered. "Maybe. And also, a bit crazy."

She put her right hand on the middle of her chest as if she could really feel the intensity of the undertaking. "Yeah, wow, I bet it can feel like a lot out there."

I let out a big sigh. "Yeah, it has been a lot. And you?"

"I'm with a group." She nodded in the direction of a few tents upslope. "We paddled from Whitehorse. This is where we stop."

"Nice, that sounds fun." I smiled as I imagined how relaxing it must feel to be in the company of others.

"Yeah. We all work together at the University of Lethbridge. It's a real privilege to be out here in this beautiful wilderness." The sunlight cascaded through the tree canopy and was sparkling off the rain droplets as they hung onto the spruce needles.

"It sure is a gorgeous place." Even with all the challenges I had experienced on my journey, I could still appreciate all of its beauty.

"I'm inspired by what you're doing. It really means something you know, this trip you're on. Especially as a woman, alone."

"Thanks, Sharon. I really needed to hear that right now. I barely made it today." I looked over at the river below as it was now awash in afternoon light, and shifted the weight of my now upright body from one foot to the other.

"I'm sorry. Yeah, that weather was rough." She furrowed her brow as if she were going to take it up with someone.

"Yeah, I felt like that rain was never going to end. And, then there was the wind storm yesterday. It took my hat!" I rubbed my hand through my greasy bangs and along the top of my head.

"Oh no. I'm sorry." She furrowed her brow even deeper.

"All good. You know, Sharon, sometimes I feel alone out there, but then I meet people like you and I'm reminded that's not the case." I smiled at her shyly.

"Thanks, Kay." She readily returned my smile. "Hey, you look hungry. The diner is still open you know."

"Music to my ears! Yes, I'm starving. Time for a burger. Talk later?" I could barely stand still at the news. I felt bad with how hurried I suddenly became, but my starving body had taken over.

Sharon nodded in understanding. "Sounds good, Kay. Enjoy!"

"I will!"

I hastily followed my nose to the nearby diner and lined up in anticipation at the take-out window. I could barely hold back my glee when it was my turn to order.

"A burger and onion rings please, oh—and a coke!"

Ten minutes later my name was called. They handed me over a burger with onion rings on a plate, along with a paper cup to fill with soda. With full hands, I wandered into the dining hall, filled my cup with dark, bubbling liquid sugar, and sat down on a picnic bench across from a young man. I started to scarf down the life-giving fats. Everything tasted exactly as I had imagined out on the river.

The young man looked over at me as I stuffed my face and smiled. He seemed intrigued by me, or possibly by my weathered disposition.

"Hi, I'm Paul."

With a mouthful of burger, I looked up from my plate. "Hi, Paul. Kay."

He asked about the journey I was on. After I gave him the spiel, I asked why he was at the Coal Mine Campground.

"I'm a geologist. My cohort and I are here doing coursework together. We're studying the geology of the area."

"Cool."

"Yeah, we're actually meeting here to watch a film."

More people started to gather around us. "Oh, okay. Do I need to leave?"
"It looks like you'll have time to finish your meal, especially at that rate." He laughed at me as I pushed a large onion ring into my mouth.

Hearing about Paul's studies reminded me of the history and ongoing gold rush I used to be faced with day in and day out at my old job. As he spoke, the ongoing stress and personal pain I had experienced in my former position over those last several years in Dawson and afterwards for the first while with Jeremy in Atlin began to open up like an old wound. I finished the last onion ring on my plate and looked up at him. "Well, I think this is where I step out. Enjoy your class!"

"Thanks, Kay. And good luck with the rest of your trip! It sounds like quite the adventure."

"Thanks, Paul. Take care!"

I smiled at Paul and his fellow classmates as I left the table. Even though I had a full belly after ravaging the delicious meal, I suddenly felt empty. It wasn't that Paul or his fellow students seemed malicious or that I could ever consider them "the enemy," but I just couldn't shake the feeling our society was blindly racing towards a vacuous end. We were reaping gold from the land with little regard for the impacts on that land, on our environment more broadly, or on future generations. I felt frustrated we couldn't seem to understand the true value of our world in and of itself. Rather, our society focused on the economic value of the "resources" our land and surrounding environment could give us. It felt painful to know we were continuing to destroy the natural world for unsustainable values. Now that I was opening up more and had spent intimate time in vast expanses of wilderness and been in deep communion with that wilderness and its beings, I started to understand the environment was not only "a provider," giving us what we needed for our survival, but also a truly sacred companion. Part of me didn't want to know this—like, I wanted to shut that part of myself down, because it was too painful for me to acknowledge and be in tune with the feelings and responsibility that went along with such awareness.

The experience I recently had on the river with the golden eagle came back to mind. *The animal clearly communicated with me, without words, a reminder of why I existed, why my efforts were worthwhile. When she looked at me directly, when she gave me attention, I finally felt like I mattered. That I was part of a bigger picture and I would not be forgotten. What could be more valuable than being told you matter?* In that moment, I came to understand the true value of the eagle. An animal who had such inherent wisdom and compassion for me as another being. Was it the world waking up around me, or was it me waking up to the world that had been there all along? Had I been distracted this whole time by keeping myself busy at work, by tiring myself out beyond recognition? It was as if the eagle had been waiting for me on her perch by the river. Waiting for my breaking point, so she could use it as an opportunity to remind me of who she really was, and who I really was.

I headed back to the campground and hit the showers and laundry. Layers of exhaustion wept off my body in the hot water and soap. Salt, like a dying sea, wicked off my skin and down the drain. My muscles sighed and expanded under the safe heat. The welts on my hands screamed as I ran my fingers through my hair, but under the rain of the shower head, even their cries washed away. As the steamy water drenched my head and shoulders, it also cleared my psyche. I felt a shift. *That's it! I'm going to start this trip anew. This time it's going to be different. I will no longer be a victim of my journey. I'm ready to fully accept and embrace my undertaking.*

After the heavenly shower, I threw all my dirty laundry in the washer and went back outside to the campground to set up my tent. As I fumbled with my tent poles, Sharon approached me.

"Hi, Sharon!"

"Hi, Kay. How're you feeling?"

"Much better after the food and shower, thanks. Like a new person!"

"You look good, much livelier. But what's going on with your hands?" She looked down at my blistered fingers as they manipulated the tent poles.

"Yeah, not sure what these things are. But they're getting worse with the exposure. Super painful."

The look in Sharon's eyes mirrored the discomfort I felt. "Do you have gloves?"

"I did, but the heavy wind snatched one from me yesterday, along with my ball cap. I was blind out there in the rain without the hat because the rain drops pool on my glasses."

"Oh geez. Hey, give me a sec. I'll be right back." Sharon wandered off to her campsite and returned a few minutes later with a pair of gloves and a pink camouflaged ball cap. "These are for you."

"Wow, thanks. That is so kind of you. Are you sure you don't need them?" I felt uncomfortable accepting such a generous gift, especially from a stranger.

"Like I said before, we're done our trip now, so I won't be needing these anymore. I have no need for them back home."

"Thanks, Sharon. These mean a lot and will honestly save me out there." I reached out and accepted the cap and gloves from her and put them with the rest of my gear. Sharon smiled kindly at me.

"I'm just so inspired by the trip you're on and am glad to help in whatever way I can."

My heart buzzed with warmth from her generosity. After putting up the tent and finishing my laundry, I was ready to tuck in for an early night. I was making up my bed, when I heard a familiar voice down at the dock.

"Haha, yeah! Wet as a duck. Give me a hand out of this floating pool!"

Derek? How could that be Derek. The last time I saw him, he was way back. Again, when he'd pulled over to see the grounded remains of the old stern wheeler, I was convinced we had parted ways for good. I left my tent and walked down towards the dock and lively chatter. A man who I didn't recognize was on the dock reaching his hand down to help someone out of a large canoe.

"Derek?" I squinted at the silhouetted canoer who was now half way up onto the dock, thanks to the assistance of his friend.

"Oh! Hey, Kay!" Derek's whole body was soaked and he looked even skinnier than usual because his wet clothes clung to his tall, thin frame.

"I can't believe you made it here. And so early too. I didn't think I was going to see you again!" Derek's friend grabbed the rope on the front end of his canoe and tied it to the dock to secure the vessel.

"Haha, yeah. The rain was driving me nuts out there! I'm fucking drenched. I figured I better push it for some hot food and a shower."

As I got closer, I could see my former travelling companion was shaking from exposure, and his face looked even more drawn and tired than it had during the time we'd spent together a few days prior. The bottom of his canoe was full of water with a few of his belongings half-submerged, half-floating on its surface.

"Man, I need to get onto dry land and eat something."

We walked up the dock to the campground and sat down beneath the large spruce trees. After pulling a few things out of the water in Derek's boat and placing them on the dock to dry, and grabbing his tent and sleeping gear, Derek's friend wandered up and peered down at him. "Hey, Bud, the diner is only open for another half hour. What can I get you?"

"Oh, awesome! Burger and fries please, and as much grease as possible!"

"Sounds good, Bud. Comin' right up!" His friend wandered off towards the diner.

"I'm so impressed you made it, Derek. I was caught out in that weather too. It was brutal."

"Yeah, I couldn't stand it anymore. I was so motivated to get off the water and call it a trip."

"It's so good to see you again." I smiled over at him and was immediately stricken by the state he was in. He looked pasty and was shaking involuntarily. "Hey, you look rough, Derek. Do you have some warmer clothes?"

"Yeah, I've got some in this Ziploc bag." He held the bag tightly as he stood up with a groan. "Time to make the change then." He hobbled towards the men's washroom.

"Grab a shower while you're at it! It's heavenly!"

I went back to my camp to finish setting up my bedding. By the time I'd finished, Derek had returned from his shower and was sitting on a stump near my camp shovelling greasy diner food into his mouth. I sat down beside him.

He didn't look up from his plate as he ate. "Feels so good to be around people again." I could barely hear his muffled voice between french fries.

"Yeah, I hear you. I feel super-relaxed being in good company. I didn't sleep at all last night. Got caught in that horrible wind storm and camped at Cyre's Dredge all by myself. It was awful."

"Haha!" Small chunks of emaciated potato flew from his mouth as he laughed. "Welcome to my world!"

"I don't know how you keep going without sleep. I felt so out of it on the water today without it. My brain was in full-on sabotage mode."

"Mm-hmm. Relatable . . ."

As Derek finished up his plate, the tension in his face lessened and he seemed to be coming back to earth. His friend wandered back and we all went down to the dock to help unload his gear and bring the canoe up into the campground. Sharon came by and chatted with Derek as he put up his tent.

"Well folks, it's time for me to tuck in for the night. I've got a big journey ahead of me." I knew the next stretch of the trip would be a new level. Very few people would be on the water between Carmacks and Dawson, and the river would separate even further from the highway and wind deep into the wilderness. There was also the infamous "Five Finger Rapids" I had to look out for.

Derek looked over at me and smiled. "Have a good sleep, Kay. I'm sure I'll see you in the morning before you head out."

"Thanks, Derek. I hope you get a well-deserved sleep."

"You know what? I think I finally will."

After drying and collecting my laundry over at the wash house, I entered my tent and tucked into my sleeping bag. I pulled out my inReach and sent my check-in to Natasha, Jane and Jeremy. "Arrived in Carmacks! All fuelled up with burger and onion rings!" Natasha and Jane responded with words of encouragement. "Way to go! You've hit a milestone!" and "Woot, woot! Enjoy those hot showers!"

But there was no response from Jeremy. *He must still be out on the land at the remote camp.* Then, I felt around the floor for my map book. Finally, I would have some bearings for the best river channels to travel from here to Dawson. I found the book and flipped through the pages until I arrived at Five Finger Rapids. I analyzed the section of river and noticed there was a distinct bend in the river just before the rapids. The waterway veered left into the rapids, where four pillared rock islands divided the river into five channels. If I stayed right, I would travel through the easiest channel to the other side of the rapids. The map book said the water was calmer on the right, with less undertow, fewer eddies and tamer rapids. The other channels, however, were much less appealing and much more dangerous. Dramatized tales of the dead were warning enough for me to take deep note of the advice, to not assume a straight run would be an easy run, and most of all, to focus my awareness and efforts on staying right. *I'm ready and prepared,* I thought, as I put the map book down and turned over onto my side. *I know what to do.*

As I lay there, a reassuring feeling swept over me. I still missed Jeremy, but felt less attached to the need for his company now that I was united with my traveling companions and surrounded by the other campers. My consciousness dissolved deeper and deeper while I listened to Derek and Sharon's voices. Then deeper still as the chatter from the neighbouring campers transformed into a soothing buzz, like the steady thrum from a beehive.

Before I fell asleep, a recent dream mingled with the thrum and chatter of sounds outside. In that particular dream, it was as though the river *of* my psyche *had jammed and then unjammed dramatically.*

It was early spring. I was back in Dawson and the river ice was breaking. The broken ice had jumbled and jammed in front of town causing the Yukon River's water levels to rise dramatically. There was a threat of flood. I was inside a big building with many rooms. I was running through hallways and doors trying to get to higher levels to evade the rising water. Eventually, I found my way through the front doors of the building to outside. I looked around at passersby wandering the streets.

"Run!" I yelled at them. "The river is flooding town!"

They didn't seem phased. Without a second's hesitation, I sped off and ran up the hill through a residential neighbourhood. Once I felt safe to stop, I turned back to look at the river. The ice was still rising dramatically and it looked like the built-up potential of the river was about to burst. I turned back uphill and ran even harder. After making it to my friend's yard, I looked back anticipating the rising river directly behind me. But instead, in an ear shattering "KABOOM" the river ice broke free from the pressure of the burgeoning water and careened downstream. The water levels retreated to the river's original breadth, and as the majority of the ice cleared, the river rejoined its dynamic relationship with the world above and flowed with a renewed vigour.

Although I was exhausted from my panicked escape of the potential flood, I revelled in the resurrection of my life before me. I felt different, lighter. All my distortions, stories and beliefs had disintegrated. They had become too heavy for me to hold, to the degree they had been threatening my life. Something had to give for my life force to return anew, and that something was a former part of myself. It was a resistant part of me I could no longer accommodate. It was the heavy cross of fears once splayed across my back. Not only did I have to give, but I also had to give up. Not in a defeated way, but in a humble communion with the truth of myself, with my very soul. I came to realize my "one and only" was the very soul that brought me here. I was here to enter more deeply into an inextricable relationship with a deeper self, who, like the river, called me to let go, or would usher me to let go all the same so I might accept, or at least blunder towards, my destiny. The destiny that awaited me downriver.

The next morning, I woke feeling the most rested I'd felt the entire trip. My body and mind had rejuvenated from the sleep, food, hot shower and good company. I was eager and prepared to start the new leg of my journey.

Suddenly, images of the dream I recalled the night before came rushing back into my mind. Similar to the fear I had experienced in the dream while running from the rising water before the river ice let lose, I had endured one of the most challenging physical and psychological periods on the trip so far directly before the moving encounter with the golden eagle and the utopia of the Coal Mine Campground. I was curious whether the rest of the dream would somehow play out in the remainder of my journey ahead. *What destiny awaits me downriver?*

I knew from here to Dawson I would be mostly alone. There were no more towns or stops where I could expect to see others, and fewer tourists did this stretch. Even knowing this, I had a new feeling of confidence in my abilities to complete the journey. As I packed up camp, I eagerly grabbed my map book, which showed the best channels to take. Finally, I would have a better sense of direction at my finger-tips. I put the book into a large Ziploc bag and placed it into the cockpit of Sugar Snap so it was easy to access.

After I had breakfast and packed up camp, Sharon and her colleague helped carry my kayak down to the docks. We placed Sugar Snap on the dock so I could finish loading my heaviest gear. Then we lifted her onto the river's surface. The water flowed gently and seemed inviting in the morning's sunlight. My friends steadied the bow and stern as I entered my kayak with a grin on my face.

I saw Derek in the campground and waved at him eagerly. "Hey, Derek! Send me off!"

He sauntered slowly down to the docks as if he didn't care I was leaving. "Oh, hey. Sure thing." He unravelled the rope, which tied Sugar Snap to the dock, and handed it to me.

I smiled back at him excitedly. "I'm doing it bud. I'm on my way!"

He smiled back shyly. "Have a safe trip." His voice was subdued and nondescript, like he was trying to downplay our goodbye and his true feelings about it.

"Thanks, Derek! Rest up and take care! It was nice to meet you!" I countered his lack of attention with over-the-top enthusiasm and hollow compliments, my own way of masking the stinging feeling now rising in my chest.

"You too, Kay. You too." He turned away quickly and headed up the dock towards the campground.

I mulled over why Derek was acting so casual about our departure. Perhaps it was his coping mechanism to distance himself from people when he knew a goodbye was imminent. Maybe it was a hangover from his training as a soldier. I felt a pang of regret in my own belly from leaving my new-found friend, and for real this time. I was reminded again of the many departures of life, the sting of loss, even as I was excited and ready for the next leg of my adventure.

The current was already taking my kayak, and I let the moving water pull me past the dock before I steered further out into the main channel. After a few paddle strokes, I looked back and waved at Sharon. She stood on the dock smiling brightly and waved back. Derek, who was nearly back up at the trees now, turned to face me and waved casually, as if we would meet again. Then he turned away and disappeared into the tall trees.

It was a gorgeous morning. The lark blue of the morning's sky was only interrupted by the occasional fluffy, white cloud, and the sun's new light reverberated in sparkles off the river. I took the bend wide into Carmacks and drifted underneath the baby blue highway bridge. I had never seen the town from the river before, and many houses and cabins, normally hidden from the road, showed their faces along the river banks. Soon after I paddled by the main townsite, the signs of people faded and once again were replaced by thick forests of white spruce. Unexpectedly, at the top of a sandy bluff to my right, I saw a small clearing where some workers in high-vis vests were standing and appeared to be surveying. They looked like geologists. *Possibly from Paul's group.*

They waved down at me from above. "Watch out for Five Finger Rapids! Make sure you stay right!"

I waved back at them. "Thanks!"

Since my night studying the map books at the campground, I had been mentally preparing myself for the infamous Five Finger Rapids. I read historical accounts of the rapids taking peoples' lives and wrecking the stern wheelers that used to travel the river. So, I knew I had to have my wits about me for this upcoming section. I continued along the river for some time, and at every bend, I consulted my maps to make sure I knew exactly where I was in relation to these impending waters. Finally, after what felt like hours but was only an hour or so, the map showed that I was on the last bend of river before the rapids. I stayed to the far right as I came around the bend, which felt like it would never end. Finally, the distinct rocky bluff formations of Five Finger Rapids appeared. As the name suggested, the rock formations split the river into five channels, which looked like water filtering through four fingers of a massive hand. Along the eastern bank, between the "pointer finger" and "thumb," was the safest channel for my passage. I steered fixedly towards this gateway. On top of the bluff along the bank, a small group of tourists at the highway rest stop peered down at me. As I approached, I saw their dark silhouettes slowly transforming into colour.

They began waving at me. "Stay right!"

I smiled up at them, even though they probably couldn't see my face. "Thank you!"

Sugar Snap's bow aligned directly with the middle of the right passage. The current of the river picked up and the water swirled around my kayak. Small, nippy waves kicked up and slapped the sides of her hull making hollow, smacking noises. As I entered the right channel, one excitable wave jumped up and licked overtop Sugar Snap's bow. At the same time, euphoric emotion consumed my entire being and I began weeping profusely. Within what felt like seconds, Sugar Snap and I emerged on the downstream side of the rapids and continued drifting on calmer, open waters. I looked back and marvelled at the obdurate rock masses that stood like guardians at an entranceway. Tears continued to well in my eyes and swam down my face, dropping in patters onto the porous fabric of my lifejacket.

I drifted.

Moving delicately, I extracted my sore hands from the gloves Sharon had given me and dipped my burning fingers into the cool water at my sides. As my fingers broke through the cool surface, a thought entered my mind. *Maybe, I can heal myself.* The thought came in like a trickle of potential, a glimmering of possibility. *Maybe, I have all I need to heal? Maybe, this all comes down to me.* I wasn't entirely sure what this message was in reference to. Sure, I had some undiagnosed physical ailments that were a mystery to me and the doctors, but did my potential for healing go deeper than that? Could it help me let go of my addiction to busyness and would it take my healing deeper still? Could it help me open the closet where I had stuffed all my trauma from abusive relationships and my childhood? Could it help me unpack all my fears about inheriting an unstable mind? And what about my sometimes-tenuous relationship with Jeremy? Would it help us heal our unhealthy patterns so we could realize our love for one another? Or, if not, provide me the assurances I might need to let the relationship go? How far could and would this spark shine into the darkness of my stored pain?

Taken aback by the potential of this healing to reverberate throughout my entire life, I pulled my hands out of the water, took off my glasses, and wiped my eyes. I drifted a moment longer and took some deep breaths, so I might accept the message.

As I put my glasses back on, my vision clarified, and I noticed something missing from Sugar Snap's bow. The broach in memory of my dog Mya was gone. It had been pinned there the entire trip. It had withstood the waves and weather of three massive lakes and the sizeable rapids of Atlin River. But, the one, small, curious side wave that kicked up in Five Finger Rapids was all it took to take her. I then realized I had become profoundly emotional at that exact same time. As the broach was swallowed up in the channel's undertows, I had experienced some kind of release.

We filled your grave with the sandy soil from an ancient lake. As soon as we placed the last shovel full, the sky opened up with the most powerful hail storm. Natasha and I ran to my cabin for cover and gazed out the front door at the torrential downfall of thick ice stones. It was as if the Earth knew our chapter in this world, yours and mine, was over. The heavens marked this ending ceremoniously with an outpour of clapping from the effervescent crowd.

I queried what of Mya I had released while undergoing the transformation through the watery gateway. Had I released my mourning and the loss of her companionship or the loss of that part of my identity that was connected to her?

Or, had I finally let go of her spirit so that she could reincarnate into someone new? After she had passed, a friend told me Mya would come back as a wolf. I liked the idea. To me the wolf was an embodiment of the wild and free, everything Mya represented to me. I could almost feel her new form beside me now, but I knew that now, instead of me holding onto her, she was free, and could come and go as she pleased. My passage through the Fiver Finger Rapids had allowed me to finally set her, and myself, free.

My body is small, warm, and furry and I wiggle in excitement to see you. You bend down and kiss me on the forehead and I try to nip your nose. Then, I scamper off to play with my pack. We sing in yips and howls to the wild as thanks for our freedom.

I allowed myself to drift for some time after the emotional ride. Physically, the waters of Five Finger Rapids were nothing compared to Atlin River or the many lakes I had paddled; however, their presence and the transformation I experienced paddling through their gateway was beyond any place I had ever experienced and anything I had ever anticipated.

Once my tears stopped and my body calmed, I began paddling slowly again with the never-ending current of the Yukon River. In a union of effort and allowing, I worked with the current around each bend. I passed through sections of the river that rounded near the highway, which ran high above on the neighbouring hillside. Once, I heard chatter from travellers at a nearby pit stop. Then the river pulled away from the highway and snaked its way through the wilderness.

I began to feel like the only person in the world, or greater still, invisible. As the current swept me along, I gazed at the river banks. Their driftwood spoke in abandoned whispers of high water. One piece of bleached wood especially caught my eye. It was light tan, similar to the others, but had a more detailed rendering and form. Its branches looked like elongated legs stretching off of an arched back that supported an alert head; the full figure of the banked wood was almost sphinx-like. It had a pie-shaped face, aiming directly out at the river. As I approached, I stared at the driftwood, mesmerized by its beauty. I continued to gaze at it as I drifted by, and watched it over my shoulder as I continued down river.

In a silent adieu, I inquired, *What are you? What are you, really?* She simply looked back at me and asked the same question, *What are you?*

I was shocked by the question, and even more taken aback that I couldn't easily answer. Her pie-shaped face continued to watch me as I floated past, and it turned in seamless unison with my movement. It reminded me of those portrait paintings with ever-pursuing eyes. Then, I saw more clearly, iridescent, yellow-green eyes and ears pinched like the tips of wet paint brushes. I shook my head in confusion as this sculpted piece of driftwood responded to my question. *I am a lynx.* She was sunning herself on the river bank in relaxed curiosity at my presence.

I sit here poised in your recognition. It is your recognition that brings me back to life. Thank you.

Drift with me for a while. I told you once you were forgotten, but I don't mean this in a harsh way. I mean this in the way you can disintegrate and not be defined, by anything or anyone. And this is important. It is important so you do not confuse your worth with anything or anyone. This must be gone. For it is what will hold you back from believing in the greater good.

There you are. You are more you now. I am happy to see this. This is a beautiful thing. You may find beauty in me and that is you.

Disintegrate. You are forgotten. This is good.

This state of deep wonderment, reflection, and a new, more foundational rearrangement accompanied me down the river, as if the lynx had put me into some kind of existential trance. I continued to paddle, losing all track of time and limitations of my body. I didn't stop to rest. I couldn't. *I've got to continue on.* And continue on I did. The miles I covered felt like an extension of my being, stretching across the meniscus of the earth. My instinctual commitment to this expansion of identity grew with every paddle stroke.

***

As I paddled with devotion, the day grew older. Dusk arrived by the time I passed Minto's RV campground perched atop the rocky, river bank. Still, the trance hadn't lifted, and I wasn't ready to stop. I saw an older couple sitting in lawn chairs at the edge of the campground just above the river's edge. They seemed out of place in the middle of the wilderness. I waved up at them to check

if they were real. They waved back and then continued to wave, warding off the evening's mosquitos. I paused to look at the map book to get a better sense of where I was in relation to the next campsite. Just passed Minto, the map showed a campsite called Thom's Location. *Okay Sugar Snap, last push of the day. Let's camp at Thom's and hope to heck there are people there for company.*

I took a deep breath and continued paddling on the peaceful water. As dusk set in, the flies danced low, daringly close to the river's surface. Suddenly, in an unexpected thwack along the bow of my kayak, a fully-grown chinook salmon jumped out of the river and blundered directly into Sugar Snap before falling back down into the water. I was shocked by this apparition from the cloudy depths. *Where there is one salmon, there must be many!* Given the time of year, there was likely an entire spawning ritual taking place quietly and invisibly beneath me. *It must be a male salmon defending his territory against my much larger green "salmon." Natasha told me once that they don't feed this time of year when they're spawning, so he can't be after the flies. What magic! Maybe he simply came up to connect? Or perhaps he brings a message?* It felt funny to me that there was an entire world below I had been floating overtop the whole trip and hadn't given a thought to. It was like an imaginary world to me, with the salmon as a curious and unexpected messenger from its mystical depths. I pondered the salmon's greeting. *Maybe I'll share a welcome to see if he has anything to say in return.* I imagined writing a letter to him to share with his world.

Dearest Salmon,

I've heard there aren't many of you left, so I am even more grateful I was able to see you. Thank you for coming up from the depths so I could know you, even just for a moment. Maybe I will tell my kids one day of how I knew a salmon. How I met a salmon who daringly flew above the water. A messenger between worlds. I hope you will still be around for my children. I hope you won't just be in tales told and illustrated storybooks.

I feel like you rose up from the depths to remind me of your life. Is there anything I can do for you? Any message you want me to share?

Yours truly,

Girl in Kayak

Dearest Girl in Kayak,

Real sorry about the abrupt hello. I thought you were a competing King and wanted to say "back off" from my territory. My mistake.

I guess seeing as you are asking, I could share a thing or two from my world here in the murky depths. It's not easy you know, making it back to my spawning grounds. I barely made it on a few occasions. Narrowly dodged a massive net out there in the ocean. They took my brother and sister there. I can still hear their cries in my inner ear. It's tough, but I am driven to keep our life going.

The rivers have been getting harder to breathe in, too much muck. Can't tell where my natal stream went. It wasn't where I left it, so doing my best here. I can barely breathe. But I live on because I am called to. It's my job, you know.

And then the heat, nearly too hot to handle in these rivers now. I have to find undercut banks and small side streams to cool off in just so I can keep swimming.

I don't want to come across as a complainer, but I'm wondering if you can pass the message along because maybe your world can do something about this? I have no idea where all these changes are coming from.

P.S.

I would love to better understand the connection between our worlds. Do you need us? Do we need you?

P.P.S.

Where are you swimming back to?

Yours truly,

Chinook Salmon

It wasn't long after the salmon's greeting when I saw a kayak beached on the river's eastern shoreline. *Must be Thom's Location! And I'm in luck, someone else is there!* I steered towards the kayak and pulled Sugar Snap up alongside. There was a small worn path leading from the rocky shore up onto a treed plateau. I followed it up into an opening where there was a large fire-ring. An older, man was sitting on a stump next to the fire pit. Further back in the bush, there was a small cabin that looked to be about half a century old. To the right, I noticed a small tent tucked away in the mature forest.

When he saw me, the man stood up with a surprised look on his face. "Hello there!"

"Hi!"

"I am Hans."

"Hi, Hans! I'm Kay, nice to meet you. Do you mind if I look around?"

"Not at all!"

Hans was a lanky man with a German accent and silver hair. From my quick assessment, he looked to be about sixty years old and appeared to be an outdoorsman given his Gore-Tex jacket, hiking sandals and fit body.

I looked towards the cabin, then back at Hans. "Have you been in the cabin yet?"

"Yes, it's pretty nice in there, but I prefer to tent it."

We walked up to the log cabin together. There was an unsigned note pinned to the door, so I read it out loud.

> Thank you to the caretakers for keeping this cabin in such good shape. We set up camp here and a mother grizzly and her cub wandered through, so we decided to stay in the cabin for the night instead of our tent. Having the cabin made us feel so much safer! The bears didn't return or cause problems, but we were still really happy to have the cabin as a safe place. Thanks again!

Hans smiled at me reassuringly as I finished reading. "Not to worry. I haven't seen any signs of grizzlies since I've been here. I think that note was written about a week ago anyways."

I smiled in agreement with his assessment. "Yes, it's dated August 15th."

The interior of the cabin was basic; there was no furniture, just an empty room with an old wood stove. Although it was clean and looked well-kept, the cabin smelt earthy from age and there was a slight tilt to the floor.

We wandered back outside and immediately something on the roof caught my attention. "Haha, that's hilarious!"

"Yes, I know."

"Spruce trees growing out of the roof like that!" I nodded up at the saplings then looked over at Hans. "Imagine what this place is going to look like in twenty years!"

"Yes, the forest will take it back."

"It sure will by the looks of it."

Hans smiled and looked over at the willows and young spruce trees growing next to the cabin.

"Hey, Hans, would you mind sharing the campsite tonight?"

"Oh! Not at all, not at all." He looked up at me and gave another welcoming smile.

"Appreciate it, Hans. I prefer camping where there are other people if I can."

"Yes, of course. It will be nice to have the company."

"Thank you so much. Well, I'll suss out a good spot for my tent then."

I wandered around the plateau and decided the best spot for my tent was near the fire-pit closer to the shoreline amongst a cluster of larger white spruce and poplar trees. As I was setting up the tent, the comment about grizzlies in the note drifted back into my mind. *I'll be fine, Hans is just across the way if anything happens.* I faced the door of my tent towards the kayaks and river so I could mobilize if need be. Once my tent and bedding were all set up, I diligently pulled out my kitchen from the kayak and set up on the rocky beach. Hans joined me as I made my dinner.

"What's on the menu tonight?"

"A box of dairy-free macaroni."

"Hmm, sounds okay. I have been eating dehydrated meals from the outdoor store I work at back in Germany. Do you want one?"

"Oh no, I've already got the pot boiling, but those sound way better. So, you came all the way from Germany to do this trip?"

"Yes. I came out here on my own to do the paddle. All the people I work with back in my city are serious outdoor adventurers, so it was no big deal to them."

"Where did you start?"

"The Nisutlin headwaters, finishing up in Dawson City."

"Oh cool. I've never been on that river system."

"Yes, it was beautiful. Much smaller though with lots of twists and turns, and bugs and wet weather."

"Oh, tough."

"But now that I'm on the Yukon, things are a lot smoother. I don't know about you, but I'm covering way more ground than I thought."

"Yeah, me too actually. Since the Yukon River, I've been moving, must be the high water. I began my trip south of Atlin, so the lakes were a different story."

"I see. Yes, I'm making so much distance that I think I'm going to stay here an extra night—take my time getting to Dawson."

My macaroni had finished boiling, so I drained the noodles and added the gooey sauce package, then stirred it all together, and started eating directly out of the pot.

"You eat that whole thing?"

"Oh, sorry. Do you want some?"

"Oh no, I already ate. I just mean, big portion."

"Yeah, I don't want to deal with the scraps. I mean, my body probably needs all the energy anyways, but, yeah, it hurts my stomach eating it all at once."

Hans' blue eyes sparkled in the setting sun as he laughed at my odd way of dealing with food. Then he looked away and down at his hands resting on his knees.

"Hey!"

"What?"

"You have similar sores to mine on your hands!" I released my left hand from the tin bowl and displayed the blisters to him.

"Oh, yeah."

"What do you think it is?"

"It's nothing."

"Oh?"

"Yes. I try wearing my gloves, but I don't like them."

"So, exposure maybe?"

"They'll go away, I'm sure." Hans hid his hands and seemed uninterested in continuing the conversation. I felt confused by his reaction, as I was so enthralled to have met someone with what looked like the same problem. I decided to let my bewilderment to Hans' reaction go and drop the whole thing. He was a stranger after all, and I didn't want to complicate our short time together and in such serene beauty.

"Yeah, I'm sure they'll go away." I scooped the last mouthful of macaroni into my mouth and felt my stomach churning from the pressure. "Gotta go!" I darted towards my kayak and rummaged in the small compartment behind the seat for the role of toilet paper. "Be right back." I dashed up the trail to the outhouse on the far side of the cabin.

When I returned, Hans was watching the sun set. The entire sky had turned hot pink and tangerine, and the colours danced across the water in a concentrated stripe ending at our beached kayaks.

I cleared my throat slightly so as not to scare him by approaching from behind. "Gorgeous, isn't it?"

"It sure is. Oh . . . I just saw a fish jump!"

"Oh cool! Hey, I just saw one too, just over there." I pointed to the other side of the sunset line on the river.

"So great."

I told him about the salmon that had broadsided the bow of my kayak earlier.

"When I first arrived here earlier today, I came down to the shore here and looked across and there right in front was a full-grown cow moose." Hans pointed across the river at some thick willows.

"Wow, cool!" I looked to where he was pointing to imagine the scene.

"Yes. I stayed really quiet and she let me watch her for a while."

"That sounds really special."

"It really was. It really was." Hans looked out across the glimmering water and smiled. The creases beside his eyes etched deeply in the shape of rainbows, echoing his genuine happiness.

As the last of the sun disappeared along the horizon, we became quiet. The undersides of our beached kayaks, which were flipped up to the sky, held onto the pinky-orange glow for a while longer, until they too grew dark.

"Well, I'm heading for bed. Another big day ahead of me tomorrow. If I don't see you before I leave in the morning, enjoy the rest of your trip, Hans."

"Thanks, Kay. It's been really nice to meet you and good to have your company out here."

"Same here, Hans. Safe travels and good night."

There was just enough light in the sky to show the way back to my tent. I wormed into my sleeping bag, put on a head-light and picked up my book, *A Return to Love*. It was the first time I'd read it since the unsettling purgatory of the Marsh Lake rest stop. That felt like weeks ago now with everything that had happened in between. My days were so full of new places, challenges and adventures, along with much beauty to take in along the way. It felt like I'd been out on the water for much longer than ten days. I sent my inReach message to the outside world, letting Jeremy, Natasha and Jane know I was safe and sound at Thom's Location. Natasha messaged back right away. "I love that area!" And then my sister Jane wrote "Glad you're safe. You are making some distance now!" *Yep, home is just around the corner*, I thought.

Strangely it was hard for me to accept that the trip was coming to a close. It felt surreal and although I was super excited to be back with Jeremy, a sticky, aching feeling arose from my heart. Was I longing for home, or was it the connections I was making along this journey that were actually bringing me closer to a feeling of home? *Will I be able to stay connected in this way and with this feeling when this trip is done?* I closed the book, took off my headlamp and rolled over into a fetal position on my right side. My mind spun in circles as I fell asleep. *I can't wait to be home. I am home. I can't wait to be home. I am home.*

I woke early to the patter of rain on my tent fly. Although I had slept most of the night, my energy was somewhat thwarted by the wet weather. The air was cold and moist and I could already feel my body temperature dropping. I knew once I set off on the river, after Fort Selkirk just ahead, it would diverge deeper into the wilderness. I also knew that from this point on, apart from a few stray individuals who might also be out on the river like me, I would have very little company to rely on if something went wrong. In attempts to stay dry for as long as possible, I decided to pack my bedding and gear inside the tent before venturing into the soggy dawn of morning.

As I finished rolling my sleeping mat, the sky lightened just enough for me to see silhouetted objects outside. I poked my head out into the spattering rain and semi-darkness and looked around. A gentle, grey light roused through the tall poplar trees along the eastern horizon, and I could make out the shapes of the firepit and tree stumps now as gentle hues of colour began to appear in the misty air.

After pulling on my thick, fleece long-johns, followed by polyester pants and fleece sweater, I then wriggled into my rain gear and pulled up my hood before stepping outside. The patter of raindrops hit the hood's beak as I walked to the outhouse. The toilet seat was cold and clammy on my upper thighs. I looked over at Hans's tent through the crescent moon cut-out in the outhouse door. There were no signs of movement. *He must still be asleep.* It didn't surprise me. He had planned to spend another night here and the weather was less than inviting.

I continued about my packing regime and carried the bags of gear down to the kayaks. *Not the best time for a picnic,* I thought, as I reached for a granola bar breakfast. I flipped and finished packing my kayak and looked around for signs of Hans, but he was still sleeping. *Farewell my friend. Thanks for the much-needed company.* I pushed Sugar Snap backwards onto the rain-pocked river. The cool water lapped up against my ankles and calves as if the river was excited to have me back. I quietly watched as the rocky shoreline of Thom's Location and Hans's kayak disappeared into the morning's mist, while I launched into the Yukon River's current.

"Brrr." Just as I predicted, I was having a hard time staying warm from starting off in the rainy weather. I tried to heat myself up by paddling hard down the river. I overextended my arms in wide circles above my head to try and pump more blood around my body, especially into my frozen feet. They were still bare in sandals and I kept pushing against the kayak's rudder peddles in unison with my paddle strokes to keep my toes from freezing.

Time passed as I ambled along the lonely river. I was only just maintaining my body temperature, but was grateful for that. The rain continued and thanks to the hat Sharon had given me back in Carmacks, I could still see somewhat through my lightly splattered glasses. I steered Sugar Snap back and forth across the wandering river trying to follow the strongest current as Derek had showed me. I smiled, wondering if these people along my journey had any idea of how much they had helped me and were continuing to help me as I paddled alone in the wilderness. Their acts of kindness continually gifted me as I carried along on my own.

Hours passed and I started to feel the wear on my shoulders and forearms from the repetitive paddling. In attempts to release the tension, I stopped paddling and stretched my arms. I pulled against the fingers of my opposing hand and pushed my palm to the sky. I was coasting along the eastern shoreline in mid-stretch when I saw him.

A small, black bear foraging in the alder bushes next to the river's edge didn't seem to notice me as I approached. Although I was very close to the shore now, maybe only three metres away, I also hadn't seen him until I was almost upon him. He was intently searching for food in the undergrowth. Taken aback by his immediate and very close presence, I froze. As I passed him quietly, for a moment it felt like I didn't exist. I was simply another piece of drift wood floating down the milky river, swirling aimlessly towards my destiny. And as I passed by him, he didn't even look up.

Once I was downstream, I looked back over my shoulder keeping my eyes on him and dipped my paddle into the water. The sound from my paddle registered, and I suddenly materialized to him. He looked up in annoyance. With a swirl of the thick water around my imbedded paddle, the bear saw me for what I was—a stinky, dangerous human. He shirked away in distaste. His body posture was so easy to read. His shoulders were tense and his facial features seized in mild distress.

Hey, there, I'm really sorry to disturb you.

Ugh. Leave me alone, would you? Can't you see I'm busy?

I'm sorry.

Some of us have to work to survive you know. I don't have time for this.

It was interesting to see how disgruntled the bear was by my mere presence. He must have been spending every waking moment eating or searching for food. And one moment wasted felt like the difference between his life and death. And maybe it was. It was late August and the winter was closing in fast. I could feel it in the air and the nights were already getting darker and longer. Soon the bear would be relying on these hard-earned calories for his long winter hibernation. And here I was, a nosy tourist, distracting his focus away from that.

I'm so sorry for the disruption.

And, I especially don't have time for your kind. This is what I imagined the bear thought in response.

I also wondered if the bear's annoyance at me somehow went deeper, as if I represented all humans. Humans—the distant relative who the bear chose to abandon many thousands of years ago. But the human was still close enough to cause frustration, like a disowned family member who shows up unexpectedly and presses all your buttons. An age-old dynamic between bear and *sapiens*. The frustration was perhaps connected to a deeply imbedded knowledge of a relationship severed on bad terms. Was the bear expressing an unconcealable frustration of being consistently and exceedingly misunderstood by people?

Intrigued by the interaction, and the virtual *non-interaction*, I mulled it over as I continued down the ever-flowing river. Instead of my inflated fear of the aggressive and predatory bear, which had visited me in my mind over and over again along this journey coming to a head through a real-life encounter, the bear I ended up seeing had no interest in me whatsoever. All the energy I had put into building my fear up about bears on this trip suddenly felt ridiculous and completely blown out of proportion. If my fears themselves had been embodied in an actual bear, the animal would have been one hundred times the size of the black bear I just saw and I would have been dealing with a much fiercer encounter.

As I paddled along in reflection, the historic townsite of Fort Selkirk appeared through a thin line of ascending mist. On the opposing bank, the Pelly River sneakily interjected into the Yukon behind the cover of thickly vegetated islands.

Fort Selkirk, at the confluence of the Pelly and Yukon Rivers, was the remnants of a historical trading town and ancestral home to the Northern Tutchone people. A few red canoes were lined up at the base of the Yukon River bank below the fort. The historic town's remaining buildings perched high above the river along a flat, open field—small cabins, some kind of a hall, and a noticeable church with a steeple. A few tourists sat eating their lunch along the river bank's edge, while others wandered through the old townsite disappearing and reappearing in and out of the small, century-old cabins.

The church's steeple struck out at me, scolding me for passing by without stopping in for a visit. *I will return another time,* I assured the rebuking God, *I've got an interview to make!* My reaction to the church wasn't from a complete admonishment of religion as I understood it helped many navigate the complexities of life and provided community. I also believed many religions were built upon the stories of real prophets and enlightened people and had no interest in judging or changing people's minds about their chosen belief-systems. However, I was also keenly aware of the damage and abuse endured by Indigenous peoples and their communities at the hands of organized religions and government policy. In addition, I couldn't turn a blind eye to how some people's interpretation of their religious doctrine resulted in societal division and even war. In some ways, I felt many of our inner conflicts and harshness towards ourselves was a hangover from our societal guilt complex bestowed to us by the "big judge" weighing out our innocence and guilt at the pearly gates. Even the concept of heaven as an afterlife, somewhere we were going to away from all the mess, rather than the life right in front of us, had some damaging effects to our relationship with the environment. Unfortunately, the belief-system that everything on the planet was put here to serve us, promoted a consumptive relationship with the environment, rather than a protective and respectful one.

The more I explored my own spirituality and relationship to my inner and outer worlds, the more I came to believe in dynamic and numerous spiritual sources. To me, the "Almighty," was more akin to a pure awareness of which we all belonged, but that did not contribute to or interact with our day-to-day existence. For a more intimate knowledge and relationship with the individual, I believed we could reach out and receive guidance and support from many sources, like spirits, angels, the natural world, and our souls to name a few. Amidst my reveries, I continued on down the swift river rocking gently side to side and digging one paddle then the other into the river's thick surface.

A short way downriver along a pronounced cliff, a small cabin greeted me from high above. It sat precariously at the edge of the cliff, alone, like a misplaced postage stamp on a fading message from humans: "People once regularly trapped and travelled this unfettered land."

After passing Fort Selkirk, even though the landscape was wild and untamed, it began to look more and more familiar, like a place I knew well, a little bit like home. Rocky cliffs jutted up from the river along its north-eastern banks. Their orange and red make-up complimented the light green leaves of the aspens lining their lower slopes. Then, a stretch of islands appeared in the near distance. The islands were covered in towering stands of sturdy aspen trees and thick bush; each had small, rocky beaches upstream and sandy beaches downstream. From an eagle's perspective, I mused, the islands must have appeared like all-knowing, ovoid eyes.

Surrounded by scatterings of driftwood that danced along the river's surface, I no longer felt like a lone paddler. The driftwood keeping me company took many different forms. Some pieces looked like small crocodiles or people floating on their backs; others looked like deer with splayed antlers or foxes with pointy ears. Some moved about the same speed as Sugar Snap and me, and I tracked them as they moseyed along peacefully to an unknown, yet certain destination.

I made my way around another bend in the expanding Yukon River and towards another large island covered in aspen trees. About 30 metres directly in front of me, another piece of driftwood ambled on the water's surface. Two pointy branch nubs extruded from a water-logged length of timber; they emerged only slightly above the water's surface. In unison next to each other, the nubs drifted across the river towards the western bank. *This piece could be big underneath, best to avoid it,* I thought, as I steered in

the opposite direction. Responsively, Sugar Snap veered to the eastern river bank away from whatever was submerged beneath the pointy, black nubs. But then strangely, the distinctive piece of driftwood seemed to follow my direction and the dark nubs also veered towards the eastern bank. *Wait a second,* I thought, in confusion. I pushed my left foot down onto the peddle beneath it and Sugar Snap quickly veered west away from the length of drifting wood. Shockingly, the nubs again copied my move. They also shifted west, as if to follow me. *What the heck is that?* The nubs were now directly ahead of my kayak and I was gaining on them.

Then, as if with some kind of awareness of my boat's presence, the nubs quickly shifted away from my kayak back to the eastern river bank. This time, the nubs did not return. They continued along a fixed path, carving through the tea-coloured water towards shore. Upon closing with the shoreline, they emerged further and began growing in size as they lifted out of the water. Below the nubs, a black, fur-laden head appeared, followed by a neck and body. The dark fur was drawn and the body appeared elongated from being completely drenched in water, but I could still make out who it was. *A bear?!?* The bear's lean limbs, accentuated by the water's plastering properties, gave a concerted push, and he hoisted his body out of the river. Then, with his wet body, he made for the cover of thick alder bushes.

Whoa, was I just in a game of cat and mouse with a bear? My body shook from this unnerving potential. *Was that bear tracking me? Or, did it think I was tracking it?* Had the bear, with its intrinsic ability, sensed my movement in the water? Was the bear confused and fearful, trying to flee my ever-pressing presence. Had I quashed its dreams simply by being there? My now-alert mind was ripe with wondering.

The island the bear was originally heading for at the beginning of our encounter offered prime forage of thick green aspen leaves, a delectable and preparatory feast for his impending winter hibernation. My presence could have been enough to throw him off from his objective of reaching the island for food, as he had returned to the mainland. I floated passively in my kayak for a while, stunned by this unique, close encounter. It was my second meeting with a bear within a couple of hours. "I feel like this is bear alley, Sugar Snap. Seems the closer we get home, the wilder it is!"

Home had a familiarity about it that I couldn't fully understand. There was something about seeing the black bears, hearing the silt fizz under my kayak, and witnessing the bluffs develop along the edges of the Yukon River. The wilder my surroundings got, the more at home I felt.

Even as a feeling of home enveloped my being while I paddled along the remote stretch of water, I continued towards my destination. As I took in my surroundings, I came to realize how different the river was now compared to its zippy Thirty Mile section off Lake Laberge. It was much wider and no longer blue-green, but rather tan in colour from the inputs of sediment along its way. As I paddled by numerous, large islands, Sugar Snap hugged their edges, where the river's current was faster. Sometimes I would see or hear chunks of the island's sandy banks dropping into the rushing water. I enjoyed looking into the water-encircled forests as I drifted by, like a tourist on a roofless riverboat peering out at mysteries of the deep jungle. I got a feel for each island as I passed and imagined what they would be like as campsites. I had never seen aspen trees in the north as large as the ones on these islands. The growing conditions must have been ideal with the nutrients provided by the flooding waters.

Every once in a while, I thought I saw an animal in these temperate jungles, but the images emerging from the thick forests would quickly reveal themselves as stationary objects, like, for example, a tall root wad strangely arranged at an aspen's base and side. It was my imagination that brought these inanimate figures to life. I looked up into the arching canopies of the aspens and marvelled at the last of the green, which would quickly be fading to yellow in the crisp fall air. I tried to absorb the colour with my eyes and store it inside myself so that I could access it during the long, impending winter.

As I became more deeply entwined in my surroundings, I began speaking the imaginary animals to life. "Elephant, rhino, lion, bear." As I named them, the root wads, stumps and warped tree trunks became the wild beasts I imagined they so badly wanted to be. It was my recognition that seemed to unleash them from their static, stationary forms, into their desired states, and for that, I imagined them grateful.

I continued speaking aloud, as if I had the power to set them free.

"And a black bear in an aspen tree." I said, gazing up at the gnarled trunk, breathing life into a bear. Unlike the other apparitions, this one responded more assertively. He reached out to a nearby tree branch and pulled leaves into his mouth. Another smaller branch snapped and dropped away from the canopy of green to the forest floor from his forceful grasp. "Oh, wait. That IS a bear in a tree," I whispered with delight. The bear was fervently feeding off the aspen leaves at the very height of the canopy. The way he climbed the tree's firm trunk with such familiarity drew me to imagine he was part of it; a dark and twisted section of the tree's bole. *I guess this game goes both ways. As I breathe life into the world around me, she too breathes life into me.*

With a smile, I turned back to the river in front of me. That had been the third bear within a few hours. "Bear alley indeed, Sugar Snap!"

As the day wore on, I decided to check my maps to plan my next overnight camp. I wanted to try for a location where there might be at least a slim chance of people, especially after the day's encounters. After flipping the pages of the map book to a few pages ahead, which had maps showing the river further downstream of where I was paddling, I found a symbol for cabins under the description "Ballarat Creek." The name Ballarat was familiar. I had heard of it back when I was doing gold exploration out of Thistle Creek seven years prior. Thistle was further downriver, but still in the same neighbourhood. From my study of the map, it looked like a small mining road came down along Ballarat Creek and ended somewhere near the Yukon River. *That looks like a safe spot to camp,* I thought, happy to see a remote sign of human life up ahead. *Shouldn't be more than an hour away.* I continued on into the early evening's light.

As it grew darker, I began feeling nervous that I wouldn't make Ballarat before nightfall. Up ahead of me, I saw a large island with a few canoes beached on its upriver spit. A small fire was letting off smoke into the dusky sky. *Should I stop?* I felt so shy when I came across people in the middle of nowhere. *Would it be rude for me to impose?* I smiled bravely as if I was relaxed and in no need of their company. And as I slowly floated past the group, I waved.

One of them waved back. "Hey! Where ya headed?"

"Dawson! But not tonight. Hoping to find a camp just downstream, maybe Ballarat?"

"Okay cool, safe travels!"

"Thanks! Enjoy your fire."

Dang it. They seemed friendly enough, and I'm sure they wouldn't have minded if I had stopped and shared camp for the night. In a way, I struggled with the idea of stopping. After spending so much time in my kayak, I wasn't even sure I could get out of it. It was like the kayak offered me a safety cocoon, a level of familiarity which I was now dependent on, and I had already drifted half-way down the island and left them with the impression that I was continuing on. So, continue on I did.

Where is this Ballarat? I pulled out my maps again and determined it should be just around the next bend in the river. In anticipation, I paddled hard to the river's northern shore so as not to miss the cabins. But as I approached where the map had shown the cabins to be, all I saw was a thick forest of white spruce. *Come on, come on. The cabins should be around here somewhere.* But only forest answered back. *Fuck. I need to stop. I'm tired, it's getting dark, and I can't go any further.* Frantically, I looked around for a Plan B. To my left, there was a sizeable island in the middle of the river. I had already passed by its upriver spit, but there was still a chance I could reach the island's shore if I paddled hard against the strong current. Without a moment's delay, I turned Sugar Snap's bow to face upstream and paddled desperately into the current. Every inch mattered and I knew that if I didn't make this island, I would be adrift much longer in the dark and unknown.

As I ferried closer to the island, I gained confidence that I was going to make it. With one last push, Sugar Snap drove hard to the rocky shoreline, and I sighed in relief at the elating sound of her hull scraping the river bed. "Made it!"

Shaking from the exertion, I pried the kayak and myself as far into shore as I could with my paddle against the river rocks. Awkwardly, I rose and stepped into the cold river water, then pulled Sugar Snap upriver and onto the beach of round stones. I stretched and took in my surroundings. The island was mostly bare, with the exception of clumps of tall willow. *Okay good, no big aspen trees, that means less food for hungry bears.* The island was one of the best I'd seen for camping, so I was pleased with my decision to make it my rest stop for the night. In addition, camping close to nearby cabins, whether they were fictional or real, gave me a strange sense of security. The familiarity of the name "Ballarat" alone also put me at greater ease. *Oh yeah, Ballarat is in the Tr'ondëk Hwëch'in Traditional Territory. That's why so familiar. . .*

I walked around the island's upstream tip and found a soft, sandy spot for my tent. I unravelled the plastic fabric of my tent, still wet from the night before, and set up camp. As I sat quietly eating my dinner, I couldn't help but scan the spruce forest on the main shore to see if I could make out the cabins. Soon the darkness closed in, so I gave up my search and ventured into my tent to send my nightly inReach messages.

"Home tomorrow?" Natasha inquired.

Wow, maybe, I thought. *I still have a lot of water to cover, I still haven't passed Thistle Creek, or the White River or Stewart River, but maybe.* I had just paddled 130 kilometres in one day, and if I were to make a run for home tomorrow, I would have to paddle 170 kilometres more. *That sounds humanly impossible, especially at this point.* Still, my interview in Dawson was set to take place in 3 days, so arriving by day's end the next day was a good goal, to allow me one day of recovery and preparation time. I was also highly motivated to get back to Jeremy. His lack of response to my messages left me wondering where he was. *Was he back in Dawson from his backcountry camping trip yet? Is he getting my inReach check-ins?* Jeremy had an aversion to technology, so maybe he wasn't messaging back because he didn't know how to, or didn't care to learn. Not knowing where he was or whether he knew where I was made me feel a little uneasy and my mind travelled to worst case scenarios. *Does he even care?*

I shuddered at the thoughts and pulled on my warm sleeping clothes and toque for the night. The air was getting cooler each successive evening. Winter was just around the corner. *Got my knife and bear spray nearby. I'm good.* I laid down and focused on the rushing sound of the Yukon River against the island's spit.

I reflected on my day as I drifted off. After leaving Thom's Location in the early hours of the morning, I had also felt myself leaving people. The last stretch of the river back home was like venturing further out to come back in.
I thought of this pattern in my life. *I have to leave to come back. Leave my comfort zone to find my authenticity and grow my soul. Leave the comfort of my home for adventure so I can return to a sense of home I had previously forgotten about or abandoned.* I was hopeful that reuniting with Jeremy after this transformative journey and time apart would be a heartwarming reunion, but the doubts from his lack of response to my inReach messages kept tugging on my loving anticipation. Would the last leg of the river back to Dawson end with a safe return home?

I'm safe. I'm safe. I'm safe. I worked the mantra over and over again in my mind until I fell asleep.

Worldly Converge

In a valley, just beyond the one where you live, where the trees rustle, and the river bubbles and froths, I can feel you unfurl from your thickets, as you grow up through death and crumpled leaves. You had been patiently waiting for the returning light, and reach out longingly towards the sparce, yet golden strands before the night returns.

As the light fades, the birds perched on your bows seem restless. As if roused by the possibility of a new era, they call feverishly and repetitively into the dark, "in heart we rise, in heart we fall, all in heart!"

Swords blacken the ridge line as you try and close off to this encounter, however impossible it is to split.

You are the hues of auburn; you are in the shades of black. You were birthed in the lap of these frightful places, and as you grow, you also decay into the earthy depths of this great magic.

The wind stops and all is still. The birds shuffle their weight from foot to foot and change their tune slightly, whistling deep into the night, "bring it all in, all of it, bring it all in."

I woke early in the morning eager to start my day. It could possibly be the last day of my adventure. I had slept on and off over the night, which was much better than most nights, probably because I felt safe on the island and had a sense of familiarity with the area.

After having a warm breakfast and packing camp and Sugar Snap, I scuttled back out into the clipping current of the Yukon River. The river continued growing in breadth, and I knew today it would be getting even wider with the inputs of both the White River and the Stewart River along my way. The sky was clear when I set off, and I was hopeful the weather would hold the whole day.

As I paddled in the morning's light, I marvelled at the bluffs developing along the edges of the river. The landscape reminded me of a time when I had perched on one of those very same bluffs several years prior as a solo labourer; the very beginning of my relationship with this land was extracting its soil to be tested for gold.

I recalled standing quiet and camouflaged overlooking the moving mass of the river. Quite unexpectedly, a red canoe came into view. Two people were paddling in peace down the centre of the river, having what I considered must be a completely surreal experience with nature. And there I stood, meanwhile, auger in hand, 50 pounds of dirt on my back, blood pulsing through my veins from the repetitive exercise of collecting bags of earth to be examined. The paddlers were completely unaware of my presence. I stood there in reflection while I watched them float by as if they were in another world.

Although I was out in the bush alone, I was very much a part of a bigger money machine. One that could lead to deals between exploration companies, investors, and corporations and, if the deals and deposits were real and rich enough, large gold mines. The soil samples I collected could be the difference between an area being left to its wildness or being developed into a fully operational mine. I guessed that the canoers I saw that day had no idea this activity was going on right beside them. I suspected they had little idea of how precious their experience of this pristine corridor really was and that it could all be changed with one bag of dirt.

As I continued to paddle, with this memory floating through my mind, the land on either side of me opened up with large deciduous trees and sprawling bars of exposed river rock. This section of river, like the bluffs I'd just passed, felt extremely familiar to me. I consulted my maps and determined it must be Thistle Creek. I had spent the summer of 2011 in this area; Thistle Creek was our exploration crew's base camp. From here helicopters had flown us all over the region and dropped us out of the sky in search of gold like scavenging ninjas.

Now, all these years later, I felt a sudden rush of love thunder towards me from Thistle Creek. I was reminded of my time here, back when I was part of the gold exploration crew—and when I had fallen hard in love. Although it was a lifetime ago, images and memories came through clearly to me as I paddled along this section of the river.

I recalled how, one day while I was out in the region collecting soil samples, I had to cut the biggest white spruce trees down to create a helicopter landing pad so my new crewmate and I could get picked up and taken back to base camp. I couldn't find a better spot close to where we were and was trying to help out the newbie by making the landing pad closer to his sample area. A chainsaw had been dropped off for me by helicopter, but, when I picked it up and pulled the cord in preparation for clearing the site, the chainsaw fell apart and its pieces disappeared beneath me into the complex forest floor. So, I used my axe and machete to get the job done instead. The newbie was slow finishing his day, so by the time he showed up, I had completed the pad as best I could and the helicopter was arriving. The pad I created was just wide enough for the helicopter to make its landing, and my hands were covered in blisters and soaked with blood. The chopper blades narrowly missed the surrounding trees along the edges of the pad, and I sighed with relief as we rose safely into the spacious sky. John, my crew-boss, sat in the front seat of the chopper beside the pilot, and after we had lifted out of the sticky situation, he turned back to me.

"Hard day at the office?"

"You could say that." I looked up from my shaking, bloody hands at his bright, smiling face and smiled back.

Months later, he finally told me that as they'd flown over to pick us up, they saw a much easier spot to create a landing site only 20 metres from the one I had chosen. He hadn't had the heart to tell me that day when they'd picked us up because he knew how much work I'd put into creating the pad and how much it would have crushed me to know another better option had been so close by. *It figures*, I thought now, as I recalled the conversation, seven years later. *Leave it to me to choose the hardest option*. Meanwhile, I thought how sweet it was that John had refrained from telling me the truth of the situation that day months previous.

One thing I couldn't quite place about my love at Thistle Creek was what came first. Certainly, I was already in love with Mya. I had brought her up from the Kootenays with me and she thrived there at the camp and out on the land as I dug for gold. She even found jobs in the camp kitchen cleaning tough dishes and warming sore feet under the dining room table. Thistle was where Mya learned how to stop running away. By giving her all the freedom in the world, she finally understood what home meant. During the first part of the summer, I lived in a tent with her. She would come back late at night from her gallivanting in the wilderness to sleep by my side. Unfortunately, she also took to swimming in the sewer pond near camp. So sometimes she would enter my tent, shake ferociously, and splatter putrid water across the tent walls and all of my belongings. While that would set me off to scolding her, it took only moments for me to forgive her occasional misdeeds. I loved her just the same.

Then there was the land, where Mya and I enjoyed long, solitary days. Was it my love of the land that had opened me up to love another? Strangely, my love for the land assured its rightful place in my heart just as I realized I was betraying her.

The sky was a vibrant blue. I was hiking along a side-slope through thick buckbrush up a narrow valley to the area of my next required soil sample. I heard it first, the thumping of helicopter blades echoing off the valley walls; then the loaded machine appeared over the hill. It flew up the valley, long-lining a drill pad from its belly. The drill was being set up nearby to carry out deeper and more permanent exploration of the site. It was the first time I had come close to the progression of the work I was doing. Up until this point, I was merely a bush rat, working alone, collecting soil samples. When I saw the drill pad, I realized my soil samples were part of the succession. I could no longer ignore that I was both in love and in betrayal at the same time.

I felt conflicted with all of these memories rushing back as I floated by Thistle. I wasn't sure what to do with any of it. My heart fluttered and dismantled into pieces, which scampered off to hide in the surrounding bush. I let some of those pieces remain there, perhaps unconsciously knowing they would return to me if needed, when needed, in right timing. Floating along the river, I was simply a witness to my past even while I paddled through the present. Where my heart, or life, would take me next was at that point anyone's best guess.

Adding to my inner confusion, as I continued along the river, I started to hear the hum of large mining equipment coming from somewhere off the river shore in the surrounding bush. I felt strangely comforted by the humanness of the mechanical noises. I craved seeing people and felt a longing for others that I had never felt before. It was reassuring to know other people were nearby while I was out on the river alone, but I also felt a welling of sadness deep in the recesses of my body. Deep down I knew if I could hear the equipment in use, it meant a mine was being developed. This also meant an impact on the surrounding land, water and air as well as on the animals that called the area home, and on my own experience with the wild.

I knew the primary reason I was able to connect in the way I did to nature, to the animals, to people and to myself on this extensive journey was because of the immersive opportunity to experience large tracts of remote and untouched wilderness. My experience would not have been the same if there were operating mines along the way. Their operations would adversely impact the transformational connections I had experienced on my journey so far. I thought back to the wildlife encounters I had had and how without these quiet, yet poignant greetings, my journey would be stripped of meaning. In a scenario of numerous mines along the river and in the surrounding bush, the wild animals would be displaced, stressed and spooked from the activity and noise. The loud mechanical equipment and processes for extracting the ore would disrupt the vast stillness of these wide-open places, currently only punctuated by birdsong and the sounds of the river. The very nearness of the mines and people working at them would alter the wild nature of the landscape and its various beings. Instead of opening to a spiritual connection with my surroundings, I would be consumed by the presence of humankind and their constant desire to take something from the land rather than letting it be as is. The very water I would be paddling on, would be polluted and the water levels changed. This would impact not only my experience travelling on the river, but also the animals relying on the water to drink, and those, like the salmon I encountered earlier at Minto Landing, who lived in it. The mines would contribute to carbon emissions and climate change from their operations and the efforts made to mobilize equipment, people and electricity to the sites as well as the shipment and processing after the ore had been mined. I tried to imagine the future for this incredibly beautiful and also gold-rich area. *What will it eventually look like? An extended mining-complex? Or will we be able to maintain the natural diversity of plant and wildlife here as well as traditional activities and tourism while developing mines at the same time? Or is this an impossible ideal?* I heard the area was rich in ore deposits, so the opening of one mine could lead to the subsequent development of many. And, access granted for one type of mining operation seeking to extract certain mineral deposits could pave the path of access for many others in search of a variety of desirable minerals within the region.

I was reminded again of the canoers years ago, whom I had watched from the bluff when I was bagging dirt for gold. They had seemed to be innocently enjoying their experience of nature, perhaps not knowing that in the background, mining development pressures were constantly brewing for the stretch of land adjacent to the river on which they paddled. Now, I was the paddler along the same river, with some measure of knowledge of how the land I travelled through was being transformed even while I journeyed. I was aware of the delicate balance at play between mining interests and development and my surrounding environment. This land was changing, and the transformation I was undergoing myself made me feel these changes in a deeper way. My mind wandered back to another moment, at Thistle Creek, all those years ago. Perhaps the infancy of my own transformation had begun while I was out on the land, exploring for gold.

I spear into your neck and as I look up, I see that your spine makes up the ridges of this gargantuan basin. I count its pointy lobes as I dance wickedly across your back, sampling your pockets of riches so one day we can come back and dig a little deeper. You must think we're nuts, I think, as I rest in a moss-laden thicket of black spruce and Labrador tea. I breathe deeply, hoping to suck up enough of the tea's aromas so I never have to leave, or return to this place. I'd rather merge with the indescribable familiarity and comfort of the pungent breeze. Chopper blades thunder overhead and echo between your ribs. Something deeper in you thuds back, maybe a heart-beat? My upper lip twitches and my tears feel sticky out here, like sap.

God, this is strange. I have never felt so much love for other people and at the same time so equally torn apart by how we treat the earth. I continued to float on the never-ending current surrounded by the deep rumbling hum of mining equipment. Then suddenly and unexpectedly, from the youthful rushing of a small creek along the banks, something whole came scuttling back to me. Each of my experiences of this area were painted with a different colour and now they were merging into a new vibrancy. My first time out here I was looking for gold, then I worked for the First Nation in efforts to find a sustainable balance, and now I was paddling through the region on a spiritual journey as a witness to it all. My very presence on the water through this shared space allowed for an integration of myself I had never known before. As I floated along the Yukon River and witnessed my seemingly disparate pasts, they merged together into the presence I felt in that singular moment. I recognized this was not a fixing, or a better understanding of what I should do or what it all meant, or how the puzzle pieces complemented or perhaps raged against one another, but rather it was a peaceful place where the two, now three, life experiences could just be together, out here on one shared river. As the distance grew between the mining equipment and me, the persistent hum of the active machinery was slowly absorbed into the sky and replaced with the fizzing of the ever-running river as it churned and swept forward beneath me.

From a distance up ahead, what appeared to be a layer of snow or ice washed into the Yukon River. I had heard of the White River being silty, but I had never imagined it would be nearly pure white. The white ash from an ancient volcano painted its waters as the river persistently cut through layers of the past. Soon I would be paddling upon a recycled past, churning and spitting up beneath and all around me. The past was actively altering the present river's course through the deposit of sediments and the slow creation of islands where previously only water flowed. *Nothing is wasted.* I mused in wonder as I arrived at the mixing zone of the two great rivers.

Bursting forth in colour the blood of my veins and the tragedy in my heart. The colours of the rainbow, arching forward with no other choice.

We were forged by the volcano millions of years ago, now trapped in the earth and dissolved into the merging rivers. We are still here! In miniature flakes of unlikely companions. Bubbling soup from a time before memory, that's where we sprang from.

The land split like the middle of my heart and cascaded open in the tumbling of your flesh. The water it worked through us and carved our bodies from the dark. We were designed to live in union, over and over again and in all forms. I see this now. Our emptiness only carries our potential to reunite with the bones of the earth.

As the waters of the White River swirled with the beige waters of the Yukon, it reminded me of a barista's latte: dark earthy brown coffee merging and churning with smooth, white cream. *Mmm, coffee,* I fantasized as I drifted at the surface of the churning, fizzy water where the excess silt tried to escape. The river was so overloaded with silt now that it broiled like soda pop against the bottom of my kayak.

With the interjection of the Pelly River earlier and now the White, I was feeling overwhelmed by the sheer volume of water I was now navigating. The river spilled out wildly across its bed, snaking around an ever-growing number of islands. In some sections, the water barely covered the cobbled riverbed, and as it flowed overtop of the stones and sediment, it formed riffles that flashed energetically in the late summer's sun. Debris loaded the river and root wads, beached mid-river, splayed just above the murky shallow water.

The river branched out extensively, offering a dizzying number of options of which channel to follow. *Luckily, I have the maps now. I would've been lost without these.* I fumbled through the pages while eyeing the river up ahead. The map book clearly showed which of the many channels was the preferred route to travel. Once I found the pages I needed, I perched the sealed plastic bag with maps inside on my lap so I could follow their directions religiously.

At this point, I was eager to get home to Jeremy and didn't want to stop for much of anything. Even peeing was a chore that I tried to hold off to the last possible second. After passing the White River, I couldn't hold my bladder much longer, but every time I tried to pull to the side of the river bank, the strong current had another plan and tore me offshore and further downriver. Finally, I was able to hang on tight enough to some bowing willow and popped a squat just outside my boat into the river. *Probably not the best etiquette,* I thought, though my body relaxed with relief.

As I continued on, the rocky bluffs returned, lining the river banks. I gazed up at their familiarity, and they spoke back to me in snapshots or images from times of my life gone by. The images reflected enraptured moments shared with loved ones, like photographs blown out of the family album and onto the greater landscape. My sisters and I sharing a moment of laughter, innocently goofing around in front of the camera as children in our new-to-us Canadian home. A faded image of my mother when she was younger, before she had children. She looked beautiful and relaxed, her face aglow with love for my father as they explored the rolling hills and pastures somewhere in England. The images came into focus momentarily, before fading back into invisibility.

Wet feet on round stones leave only trace footprints which dry and disappear.

As I flowed next to the bluffs, I first saw her ears, perhaps too close together, dark slate, with skiffs of light ash. "Mya?" Then her eyes pierced through the earth, from light glancing off of smooth slate edges, the same hue of grey-blue I had painted my living room walls back at the cabin in West Dawson. Next, I saw a snout of mottled spots, catching the ebb and flow of light and dark in such a unique pattern that it could have only been worn by one soul. Another image appeared: It was me, gazing at Mya with love, and with a knowing beyond my own discomforts, that we would certainly meet again.

I walk the bluffs at night, hoping to find you there. Maybe a glimpse of your white tail tip, flickering in the dark. But instead, the moon's light is there to greet me. The moon listens to me wail about my loss and tells me not to worry because you will return.

The Stewart River joined in as I continued to paddle, now in a hypnotic stupor. *Thank goodness for this weather.* The skies were clear and the air was relatively warm. The weather seemed to be supporting my quest to continue onwards and try for home. I approached a noticeable bend in the river with large, craggy bluffs marking a shift from north-west to north. I gawked up at the bluffs as I passed by. There on the narrow cliff's edge stood wild sheep, an ewe and lamb grazing together contently. The lamb noticed my approach and bounded to her mother for protection. Seeing these strikingly white animals in the middle of the quiet wilderness was like being graced by jewels. The sheep gifted me with a short burst of energy, but my fatigue quickly took hold again.

I had probably already paddled over 100 kilometres and wasn't sure I could muster the energy to continue. The river had grown tremendously from the addition of all the confluent rivers, and I was losing track of its main current. *Oh my God, I don't think I can keep going like this.* The wind picked up and blasted me in my face, arms and chest. *And now, I have a head wind. I need help! Where is this current?* In my delirium and exhaustion, it felt like I was paddling in cement, like I was making no progress at all. My arms alone were doing all the work, and I couldn't bear the physical strain much longer.

I squinted my eyes against the glaring sun refracting off the water in efforts to try and read the river's surface. *Which way to go?*

Then, out of nowhere, a small rainbow appeared ahead of me on the river and slightly to my right. It wasn't raining, so I couldn't understand what was making the rainbow. *Maybe there's moisture in the air? But the sky is clear.* The small rainbow hovered just above the river's surface and ended on a section of water near the river's bend. *Well, I asked for a sign, maybe that's it!* I used my last remaining strength to push forward towards where the rainbow was hitting the water. Then, suddenly, the rainbow disappeared. Still, I was able to keep track of where it had met the river's surface moments before, and I continued to paddle in that direction.

As soon as Sugar Snap's nose met the rainbow's shadow, a strong current gathered beneath us and pushed us forward with surprising momentum. "Well done Sugar Snap! We're back in the flow!" I felt elated I was being assisted once again by the main current. I was also awestruck that the same invisible force I had encountered numerous times before on this journey had showed up again when I needed it the most. *When I open up, I see I'm not alone after all.* I couldn't help but feel revitalized by the constant reminders that I was not doing this journey on my own; it was, and had been, a team effort. In an immediate response to the support, I regained my energy. Back in my rhythm, I forged ahead with the swift current. It felt like we were going home together.

At this point, the daylight was fading fast and according to my maps I was still about 50 kilometres away from Dawson. I finally pulled over onto a small gravel island and took one of my only rest breaks of the day. I had been snacking in my kayak throughout the day, but hadn't stopped to stretch my legs. I turned my flip phone on to look at the time. It was 8 pm. *Shit, it's late.* I unwrapped some cheese strings and scarfed them down with some dry pepperoni sticks and crackers. I gazed downriver to see if I could catch a glimpse of civilization. But instead, all I saw was more water, rocks and trees. *Well, I should send an inReach check-in, but this time, I'll say I'm going to keep paddling for a bit longer.* Natasha promptly replied, "Way to go! Nearly home!" *Maybe she is right.* My heart wanted so badly to make Dawson by nightfall so I could see Jeremy, but my mind scoffed at the preposterous proposition. Besides, it was already getting dark and I had a long way yet to go, and there was still no response from Jeremy to my inReach messages. With a mixture of emotions, I strapped the headlight around Sharon's pink-camo hat and pushed the worn-out body of Sugar Snap back out into the dark, cool water. I had to pep-talk my body to get back into the confines of the cockpit, after which I shifted my agitated joints back into position.

Not much longer, you're doing great. Here we go.

I reached forward and patted Sugar Snap on the side of her hull at the bow end of the vessel. "This could be our last push, girl."

She had been such a trusty steed on this adventure. Without her agility and stability, I wouldn't have made half the distance I had. The breadth of her belly also kept me from being beached in storms on Lake Laberge, and with a lesser vessel, I surely would have capsized in the tumbling waters of the Atlin River.

"If it wasn't for you, I might not be here." I smiled down at Sugar Snap.

Her green hull glowed as she humbly reminded me, "And you, and them."

I placed my paddle into the swift current and we returned to the continuously flowing river. Darkness rolled in, subtle at first, as we continued past rounded mountains, creek gullies and cliff faces. Around every river bend, I anticipated the lights of Dawson, but instead I found more river and more wilderness. As Sugar Snap and I passed closely by islands to our port and starboard sides, the islands enquired, "Would you like to set up camp? I have a nice beach here for you. You could have a campfire. I will look after you. You look tired." I heard them ask, as if they had spoken to me out loud.

In determination, I clenched my paddle tightly and dug it deep into the dark water. "We are sleeping at home tonight, but thank you."

With an adjustment of my headlight, I looked down at the final few pages of my map book. I couldn't believe my eyes as the reality sunk in that we were on the last stretch to Dawson.

"Sugar Snap, just around the bend!" *Maybe I will be with Jeremy tonight after all.*

As we emerged past a treed hillside and out into an open stretch of river, the now-dim view opened up to unveil one of the most familiar and highly anticipated landmarks of my journey.

"Moosehide Slide!"

Moosehide Slide was a large, millennia-old landslide at the north end of Dawson City. It was a signature landmark that had guided many a weary traveller, during present-day, the Klondike Gold Rush and in the long-distant past. But this time, the slide I thought I knew so well looked entirely different than I remembered it. Instead of the familiar shape of a moosehide, the beige sweep of loose rock formed into a large face. Shocked at what I saw, I closed my eyes and opened them again. One half of the face was a woman's and the other half a wolf's. With darkness quickly falling, I kept closing and opening my eyes to correct what I saw, only to be greeted by the same part-human, part-animal visage. I rested my paddle across the bow of my kayak momentarily and contemplated what was going on with me and around me. *Did the world just transform, or am I the one transformed? Or, are we changing together?*

As I gazed over at the face, I wondered who she was. She looked beautiful with a wild strength about her and an expression that embodied a deep wisdom and knowing. There was something about her that evoked a feeling of inner peace deep within me, like the comfort of being with a close friend.

In my pause, the river's current kept Sugar Snap and me moving. Eventually, I came to and realized seeing the slide meant I was close enough to Dawson that I might have cell service. *I should get in touch with Jeremy,* I thought as I felt for my flip phone in my lifejacket pockets. Once I had it in my hand, I turned the phone on and saw two bars in the top left corner of the small screen. *Yes! I'm in range!* I selected Jeremy's phone number and dialled.

It rang a few times before he answered in an inquisitive voice. "Hello?"

"Babe!"

"Kay? Is that you?"

I felt his smile slide through the airwaves to where I sat in Sugar Snap. "Yep! And guess what?"

"What?"

"I can see Moosehide Slide!"

"What?!?"

"Yep!"

"Wow."

"I'm almost home!"

"What?!? I can't believe it!"

"Haha, surprise!"

"When you checked in yesterday, you still had so far to go!"

"You weren't responding so I wasn't sure you were getting my messages. You didn't get my last inReach message from today?"

"Oh. . . no, sorry. I haven't been watching my phone."

"Oh, okay. Well yeah, I was feeling pretty motivated to sleep in a bed tonight, with you."

"Aww, Babe."

In the background I could hear familiar, old-timey, piano music. "Where are you?"

Jeremy hesitated a moment before replying. "Gerties . . .". Turns out he was at Diamond Tooth Gertie's, for a night out on the town.

"Oh. Sorry to ruin your big night out." I felt a sting in my chest as my heart threw itself on the trigger. *Why is Jeremy out partying while I am giving it my all to make it home? Does he not care about how hard I am trying to get back to him? It's like he doesn't miss me at all, or isn't at all worried. Sounds like he is having more fun without me around.* The thoughts rushed to my mind without censor. I had just travelled a 170-kilometre day solo, my longest distance yet, after kayaking a huge distance geographically and otherwise on my own before then; I was on the border of delirious, completely exhausted, even in my exhilaration to be home, and had hoped Jeremy would be on the edge of his seat awaiting my arrival.

"No, no, I was just going to play some cards."

"Okay well, I'm making the push to come home, but I don't want to interrupt your fun."

"Don't be silly. We'll meet you at the docks when you come in."

"Okay. I'll text when I'm closer."

"Sounds good. Wow. Okay."

". . . I love you."

"I love you too, Babe."

I hung up, turned the phone off again and tucked it back into the plastic baggie in my lifejacket pocket. I felt frustrated by the conversation with Jeremy. My reaction to him was such a contrast to the euphoric experience I was having with nature. I looked back over at the slide, worried the face had disappeared along with my elevated mood. But she was still there, half-woman, half-wolf, staring straight back at me. And even when the hillsides changed and blocked my view of her, I could still feel her there, and she would reappear on the other side of each bend.

Around each twist and turn of the river, I rocked side to side in my kayak in rhythm with my paddle strokes. I thought I was only moments from Dawson, but instead the river continued. I whisked past a series of islands and finally saw the lights of the first house. It was perched on a naked hill at the onset of Sunnydale, a small farming community across the river from Dawson. The house lights up to my left glowed orange through large windows into the growing darkness.

Then, the yellow twinkle of the sodium lights of town danced out at me from the night. Drawn to their excitement, I continued eagerly towards them. To my right, a small cabin quietly greeted me from the shores of Tro'chëk, the Tr'ondëk Hwëch'in's historic fishing camp. Then, just beyond that, the rushing of water from the Klondike River where it entered the Yukon. I felt a little nervous about approaching the Klondike in the dark, so I steered further out into the Yukon's main-stem so as not to get swept into the Klondike's lively waves. As I passed by the south end of town, I heard the two rivers colliding in the blackness of night. I could make out glints of light from town splicing across the Klondike's giddy surface as her waters entered the Yukon. Once downstream of the confluence, I steered back towards town and searched for the docks.

Flashes of light bounced around in the dark near the water's edge and I heard a familiar voice.

"Kay! Over here!"

I followed the light and voice with great anticipation. Two silhouetted figures stood on the dock, and as I approached, I saw that one of them was wearing a headlamp.

"Hi!" My voice squeaked from underuse and I paddled closer still. The masculine figures walked off the dock and met me just downriver at the boat launch.

"Babe?"

"Jeremy!" With one last, triumphant paddle stroke I hit the shore with an abrasive thud.

I could see now he was with his brother Stephen. There were no crowds to greet me; the town was asleep to the grand finale of my undertaking. I was glad for the timid welcome, as I was so completely exhausted and disheveled and somewhat embarrassed of my state.

Jeremy grabbed the front tow handle of Sugar Snap and pulled us further up onto shore. Stephen held the kayak as I slowly exited with Jeremy's assistance and found my legs standing on dry land. I stood there shaking in the dark. Jeremy held my hand and I winced in pain as his fingers ran over my sores.

"How are you doing, Kay?" He turned off the headlamp on my forehead and pulled me in close. As he held me in his arms, I soaked up his warmth and absorbed a humming from his heart. During our embrace, I noticed how differently my heart felt compared to its walled-off nature at the beginning of the journey, and well before that. It felt inviting, as though I had infinite space to receive his love and unlimited capacity to give him love. There may not have been a crowd to greet me, but Jeremy's embrace felt like the biggest homecoming of all.

The homecoming back to Jeremy and Dawson was really just the beginning of something new. I had just completed the journey of a lifetime, and I was pleased the fundraiser I'd organized would have the funding I'd hoped for to help support the First Nations' leadership scholarship I felt strongly about. I also looked forward to sharing my good news of arrival with my friend Natasha, and others who had been connecting with me through inReach. Meanwhile, seeing Jeremy again, and taking in both his pride in me and his concern for my well-being felt good. I felt his support for my accomplishment, for the journey I'd been on, along with his genuine happiness to see me again. I soaked in his affection the night upon my return. We were together again, and while I'd questioned our togetherness in the past and at points along the paddle back to Dawson, it felt right and good to be with him again. Meanwhile, I had a job interview to attend two days hence. I hadn't yet begun rehearsing for how I might approach that, but I knew the new position was also important to me. I'd taken my time away from work, I'd paused, returned to a simplicity of living, and then navigated across 1000 kilometres of wilderness, largely on my own, though with the help of many. A journey that had begun out of a sense of inner desperation had transformed into something much more expansive, inclusive, and revelatory.

Now that I had had the perspective of traveling that distance on the interconnected waterways, I could truly appreciate Dawson as a blip of humanness surrounded by a great expanse of powerful, wild beauty. The stark contrast between the bustling town and its surrounding wilderness reminded me of the relationship I had experienced between the islands enroute and the Yukon River. I had witnessed this relationship between land and flowing water as one of two seemingly different worlds colliding and then expressing themselves in a continual dance with each other. I thought of my relationship with Jeremy, also, and how it progressed in a similar dance as the islands with the river, in a state of continuous intermingling, collision, and recreation. I wondered where this dance would take us next.

After having returned from the wilderness, it felt strange being back around people. Going out for breakfast to a bustling restaurant in town the next morning, even given my ravenous hunger, was a jarring experience. I felt like I didn't belong truly in either world, rather I existed somewhere in-between.

"Maybe this is where my magic happens?" I muttered under my breath as we drove into town and I looked out the truck window at the houses and people busy about their day. Jeremy overheard me and turned to me with a smile.

"What was that?"

"Oh, it's just so amazing that a drop of water from the O'Donnell River can make it all the way here and out into the Ocean you know."

"It sure is, Love. It's an amazing thing."

Epilogue

I would like to offer my sincere gratitude to the collective of people, animals and elements that assisted me along my kayaking journey. I wouldn't have been able to do this trip without you. Your presence coloured and excited my travels and your assistance encouraged and saved me. You were the inspiration for this book and I am forever grateful.

Jeremy Lancaster, Natasha Ayoub, Jane Linley, "Burt" and "Andy," the loon on Atlin Lake, the moose and calf on Taku Arm, the couple with dog in boat on Tagish Lake, the gull on Tagish Lake island, the supportive wind on Tagish Lake, the cloud apparition on Tagish Lake, the kindness of strangers at the Tagish Campground, the Beaver on Marsh Lake, the Alaskan in Whitehorse, the "greeting man" in Whitehorse, "Derek" from Lake Laberge to Carmacks, the Golden Eagle near Carmacks, "Sharon" in Carmacks, the Lynx, the Chinook Salmon near Minto Landing, the many bears (real and imaginary) along the way, the wild sheep on the bend to Dawson, the Rainbow on the Yukon River, the wolf-woman visage of Moosehide Slide, Sugar Snap, and, of course, Mya.

Stubborn? Well, one needs a bit of stubborn to get things done.

Brave? Is bravery only in the face of real danger?

Adrenaline seeker? No, not really.

Describing Kay won't be easy, nor the trip, as I am linguistically challenged whereas Kay has proven a champion.

I am completely in awe to see the process and completion of this book and its artwork that Kay dedicated herself to. It equals the strength we needed to push through all the hardships of this described adventure.

All that paddling, setting up and repacking camp every day, fighting wind, water and pain, and one's own doubts—pales in comparison to watching a dedicated person express the experience in words and paint. I sat for a day thinking of a picture to describe the trip—or any part of it, and nothing came to me.

I watched Kay struggle and spill as she took the memories and feelings of a journey made years before and displayed them for others to absorb and relate to. The undertaking was huge—thinking of, deciding to, planning, starting, and enduring the trip and now completing this book. Nothing short of impressive.

The trip was tough and beautiful.

Come to think of it, a little bit like Kay.

Jeremy Lancaster

In Gratitude

The journey of creating this book has been a significant undertaking and, in some ways, even bigger and more challenging than the kayaking journey itself. I took a deep dive to create this book, and though difficult at times, the experience was ultimately a healing one.

A sincere thank you to each and every one of you who have stood by me and my creation in our various stages of emerging. You have supported us in various ways, from editorial reviews to cheerleading to energetic realignments. Some of you were with there with me for the long haul, while others gave me pivotal advice at key moments along my journey. Some of you encouraged me to start, while others encouraged me to keep going. In return for your generosity, may you accept this completed expression as my most genuine and heart-felt thank you.

Though not an exhaustive list, some of your names are mentioned below in recognition of your support. And to my other family members, Cathy and David Linley, Catherine Linda Apps, Ruth Linley, and Emma Linley and to anyone else I missed, my sincere gratitude. If you are reading this book, please know you are one of my dear supporters.

Jeremy Lancaster—I have to give you your own line. Thank you for providing me the space and creative freedom I needed to follow the dream of this book all the way to completion. In return, I give you a starring role.

Amanda Moffatt, Alana Marie Arnold, Mo-Caley Verdonk, Chris Clarke, Natasha Ayoub, Rhea Lewthwaite, James Roberts, Katie Pearce, Andrea Chapman, Jane

Linley, Naomi Raven Borisenko, Marjorie Logue, Kathryn Ellis, Dan Brown-Hozjan, Veronica Verkley, Monina Wittfoth, Robin Westland, Marielle Veilleux, James Winegarden, Karli Schram, Nathalie Claing and the pups, Rhoda Merkel, Nancy Maides, Breanna Lancaster, Kim Melton, Meg Walker, Ruth Lera, Mia Hoffmanova, Elizabeth Gorman, Heather Dougan, Chantie Nordlund, Wendy Gray, Zandria Ash-Lawrence, The Goddesses of Light, Susan McCarthy, Elissa Mickey, Manu Keggenhoff.

A big heart-felt thank you to editor Barbara Kmiec whose considerate and supportive review and resonant suggestions helped me more fully develop the content of this story. And thank you to Susan Thompson and Jaclyn Killins for their generous and diligent proofing and editing support. Also, a big thank you to Collette Sadler, the talented interior book designer from across the world, and to my dear and close friend Katie Pearce for helping with design decisions and book cover design. And thank you to my writing mentor Sarah Sheard, with the Humber Creative Writing program, for nurturing my seedling of a story to grow.

A big shout out and thank you to Esteban Timpany Engasser for your amazing photographs of my paintings (the illustrations in this book), as well as my bio photo.

Oh, and last but definitely not least, to my four-legged fury friends (Junip a.k.a "Nip Nip, or "Nippers"; Diamond in the ruff, a.k.a "Diamond Dog" a.k.a. "Dimey" a.k.a "Ol' Man"; and Tin, the wilder half of "Tin-Tina" a.k.a "Tinny" or "Wolf Girl") and the two-legged feathered ones (Love you, Mika and Skye!), thank you all for keeping me grounded throughout this creative process and for helping me create from my heart.

About the Author

Hey Nippers! Down in front!

Kay Deborah Linley was born in England in 1984 and moved with her family to British Columbia, Canada at the tender age of three and a half. To heal from the challenges of her childhood and young adulthood, Kay developed a deep, spiritual connection with the natural world and a love for creating. Always searching for the highest perspective, in earlier days she delved into various kinds of work to better understand our social and environmental issues. She worked as a tree-planter, environmental advocate and plant ecologist on one hand, while on the other, as a labourer in saw mills, the oil patch and gold exploration. As she explored the various aspects of these external issues, she came to learn about the predominant role our inner worlds play in both creating and reflecting our societal divisions and environmental degradation. Kay has a complex and dynamic nature and has spent most of her life exploring seemingly unrelated worlds. This is shown in her various academic and career achievements and artistic expressions. She accomplished a masters in public policy, an undergraduate degree and diploma in natural resources, and attended art school. After taking the bold step to move to Yukon, Canada on her own, Kay gained invaluable experience working for the Self-Governing Yukon First Nations in land and resources management, land use planning and modern treaty implementation. Kay currently lives in Atlin, British Columbia, Canada with her partner Jeremy and their three dogs and fifteen chickens. *Paddling Back to Us* is Kay's first book.

www.ingramcontent.com/pod-product-compliance
Lightning Source LLC
Chambersburg PA
CBHW061129170426
43209CB00014B/1710